P

THE
TOWN & CITY
GARDENER

1992

Plants & Gardens, Brooklyn Botanic Garden Record (ISSN 0362-5850)

is published quarterly at 1000 Washington Ave., Brooklyn, N.Y. 11225, by the **Brooklyn Botanic Garden, Inc.**

Subscription included in Botanic Garden membership dues ($25.00 per year).

ISBN # 0-945352-74-3

WHO'S WHO

NINA BASSUK is director of the Urban Horticulture Institute of Cornell University. For over a decade she has concentrated on improving the lot of town and city trees in America and abroad.

ROBERT BEALE, a "city farmer," raises heirloom and modern vegetables, herbs and roses on his penthouse terrace. His family has been farming in Virginia for about 19 generations.

RUTH ROGERS CLAUSEN, co-author of *Perennials for American Gardens* (Random House, 1989), is a garden designer and lecturer. She formerly headed the School of Horticulture at The New York Botanical Garden.

KEN DRUSE is author of *The Natural Shade Garden* (Clarkson N. Potter, Inc., 1992) and *The Natural Garden* (Clarkson N. Potter, Inc., 1989). He is a contributing garden editor of *House Beautiful* magazine.

NICOLAS H. EKSTROM is co-author of *Perennials for American Gardens* (Random House, 1980) and a landscape designer and lecturer. Since 1977 he has been a director of the Horticultural Society of New York, and was Chairman of its 1992 Flower Show.

PATTI HAGAN is the gardening columnist for *The Wall Street Journal* and a regular contributor to *HG* magazine. In addition to her own Brooklyn wildflower garden she is responsible for several wildflower meadows in public areas of New York City.

ANNE HALPIN is the author of several books including *The Window Box Book* (Simon & Schuster, 1989) and *The Year-Round Vegetable Gardener* (Summit Books, 1992). She is responsible for various private gardens on eastern Long Island.

TED MARSTON is co-author of *Annuals* (Publications International, 1989). A past president of the Garden Writers Association of America, he heads a horticultural communications firm in Kirkland, Washington, where he tends his own small garden.

BILL MULLIGAN is author of *The Complete Guide to North American Gardens* (Little, Brown and Company, 1991). He is a lecturer and designer with a special interest in garden architecture. His latticework structures have repeatedly won gold medals at the New York Flower Show.

DEBORAH A. REICH is co-author of *The Complete Book of Topiary* (Workman Publishing Co., Inc., 1987). She is a lecturer and head of her own landscape design and topiary company.

MARY RILEY SMITH is author of *The Front Garden* (Houghton Mifflin, 1991). She is a landscape designer based in New York City.

VIRGINIA STRATTON researched and identified the plants in Childe Hassam's paintings of Celia Thaxter's garden for the Isles of Shoals exhibit. Her own garden is in Aurora, Colorado, where she is a book reviewer for the Denver Botanic Garden Library.

LAWRENCE B. THOMAS is the founding Chairman of the Manhattan Chapter of The American Rock Garden Society, and editor of its newsletter. His own rock garden is perched on an eleventh floor terrace in New York City.

LINDA YANG is author of *The City Gardener's Handbook: From Balcony to Backyard* (Random House, 1990) and a garden writer for *The New York Times*. Her own plot is five blocks from Rockefeller Center in New York City. She is guest editor of this handbook.

PLANTS & GARDENS

BROOKLYN BOTANIC GARDEN RECORD

THE TOWN & CITY GARDENER

VOL. 48, NO. 2, SUMMER 1992

HANDBOOK #131

FRONT COVER AND BACK COVER:
PHOTOGRAPHY BY KEN DRUSE

Even if you till a few feet of backyard or a cluster of containers on a rooftop, balcony, patio or deck, you can still have a garden that is lush and colorful.

FOREWORD

So you don't have a three-acre homestead off a winding country road. There's no need to apologize. You can still hold your head high among fellow gardeners even if you till a few feet of backyard, or a cluster of containers on a rooftop, balcony, patio or deck. That's really the only space you need to grow stately flowers like phlox, willowy vines like clematis, delectable herbs or vegetables, and even a small flowering shrub to greet each season in a different garb.

I've discovered that it's simply not true that "real" gardeners are found only on expansive rural acres or large suburban sites. In recent years, more and more of us hopeful folk are thrusting our trowels into smaller and smaller plots — not only in cities, but in retirement communities and condominium apartments that have sprung up at the edge of town.

Since too few books and articles are written specifically for us, we are often con-signed to useless scraps of information — or worse, proclamations that are misleading or just plain wrong.

This handbook, however, planned specifically with town and city gardeners in mind, shows there's no need for small gardens to be either barren or boring.

Here you will find an encouraging introduction not only to the range of superb flowers, herbs and veggies that are possible, but a sampling of rock garden plants, topiary and small weeping trees that are useful, too. Here also are suggestions for coping with shade or drought, creating a mini-meadow, sculpting a polite hedge screen, improving a front door or windowsill and adding a touch of architectural style.

I refuse to allow my own minimal space to dampen my enthusiasm for making a garden. And neither should you.

LINDA YANG

GUEST EDITOR

In the city garden as well as the country garden, the key to success is choosing plants and a style that fit your conditions.

FINDING A WAY THROUGH SHADE

BY KEN DRUSE

Town and city gardeners have to put up with a lot. There's pollution, soot, traffic and neighborhood noise. The most common lament, however, is a lack of light. "What can I grow in the dark," they ask? No ornamental plants that I know. But what is this "darkness": Is it shade cast by a neighboring tree; one or two hours of sunshine before buildings block the light; or sunless bright light from above? A shaded city garden open to the sky may actually receive more light than a country space blackened by a canopy of tree leaves. You might think that compiling a list of shade-tolerant plants would be the first order, but in city or town gardens where space is limited, the "program" is paramount.

The many shades of green are the foundation of the shady garden.
Here, Japanese painted fern, *Aquilegia* and *Rodgersia* combine strikingly.

The program is the first thing landscape designers and architects address — the particular needs of the people who will use the space. What are you going to do in the garden? Will there be a space for outdoor entertaining, cooking or eating; a spot for relaxing; or a sandbox and swing set? If you are a sun worshipper, you'll want to locate your patio where the sunlight falls. Entertaining spots are usually closest to the house. If you are a plant collector, as I am, the elements must fit in and around the program's primary directive — spaces to grow plants.

Few "cities" are born these days (new townhouse developments notwithstanding), so you probably will have inherited a plot with some landscape history. Look at your location. What grows there? Behind my 1873 Brooklyn brownstone, I found several rose-of-Sharon, two old hydrangeas, a few hostas, self-sown petunias reverted to the magenta of their unhybridized ancestors, roadside daylilies and plenty of New York asters — what most people would call "nothing." I had to start over — my new/old backyard might as well have been wilderness. For my program, I wanted: a waterfall and pool spanned by a footbridge, a raised area for seating, an arch on which to grow vines, a patio for entertaining with a meandering path to a raised area for casual seating, and generous planting beds to grow the myriad plants I yearned for. The one thing I didn't want was the mature maple growing in my neighbor's yard just to the south, which plunges my garden into darkness through much of the growing season. I plotted and planned and plotted the garden's design, making numerous drawings to scale.

After you have made a list of the things you would like to do in your garden, determine how much or how little light you have for plants. The amount of light that reaches the garden will change every day of the year. Some city gardens that receive no

The lack of sun in many city gardens presents the opportunity for a woodlandlike setting with shrubs and wildflowers of the forest understory.

Town gardens are most striking when they blend formal elements such as this brick archway with informal plantings.

Hosta species and cultivars and a variegated *Euonymus fortunei* tolerate shade and add contrasting leaf texture to the garden.

sunlight at all in winter may bask in six or seven hours of direct sunshine in June when the sun is almost directly above. South-facing gardens have the most sunlight, with west-, east- and north-facing gardens receiving less and less. East and west gardens have the same number of hours of sun; however, west allows for more sun-loving plants than east because the heat of the afternoon has an effect on growing plants that seems to be a bit like more sun. But eastern exposure can be kinder to plants. Just ask southern gardeners who find that their best gardens are cool shade gardens. One look at a hosta gasping for moisture lets you know what happens to a shade plant that is sheltered until 2 p.m. when laserlike sunlight hits the leaves.

Catalogs often recommend plants for partial shade. That is considered about six hours of direct sunlight — not what most of us imagine as shade. However, if you think of the daylight hours of summer as being fourteen hours long or more, you can see how this is considerably less sun than "full sun." From partial shade's four to six hours, there is less and less light until we come to what might be called deep shade: no sun at all, and very little light, perhaps against a north-facing wall in a

Lavender hosta blossoms blend with a mass of impatiens
in this handsome shade garden.

shaded garden, or under steps or stairs. Between these extremes, there might be what we call simply "shade." There is little sun but often bright light from above or reflected sunlight from nearby walls.

You may be able to adjust the light conditions to some extent. If a neighbor's tree limbs spread over your garden, you are allowed by law to remove any or all overhanging branches. Or, if there is a venerable oak in your backyard, for example, remove the lower branches to let in more light. You can also enhance the available light by painting walls white or a light color, and by strategically placing mirrors around the garden. I have one mirror sealed in an arch-shaped frame that fools visitors into thinking it is an opening into another garden space. Its purpose is to reflect light to a lilac and encourage a few flowers from this sun-lover.

To achieve success choose plants and a garden style that fit your conditions. But in our case, the soil *should* be based on nature's. Shaded soil is moist and airy — filled with organic matter. The plants living there have wide-spreading roots that run freely through the open medium. The soil has been enriched over time with yearly falling leaves. A good medium would con-

....

Acanthus mollis	Bear's-breech
A. spinosus spinosissimus	Bear's-breech
Actaea pachypoda	Baneberry*
Adenophora confusa	Ladybells
Adiantum pedatum	Maidenhair fern*
Adonis spp.	Adonis
Ajuga reptans	Bugleweed*
Anaphalis triplinervis	Pearly everlasting
Anemone spp.	Windflower, anemone
(woodland species and summer-blooming hybrids)	
Angelica archangelica	Wild parsnip
Arisaema spp.	Jack-in-the-pulpit*
Arum italicum	Arum
Astilbe spp. and hybrids	False spiraea
Athyrium nipponicum 'Pictum'	Japanese painted fern*
Begonia grandis ssp. *evansiana*	Hardy begonia
B. semperflorens	Fibrous begonia
Bergenia cordifolia	Bergenia
Chelone lyonii	Turtlehead
Cimicifuga spp.	Bugbane
Corydalis lutea	Yellow fumatory*
Cyclamen spp.	Hardy cyclamen*
Deparia acrostichoides	Silvery glade fern
Dodecatheon spp.	Shooting star
Dryopteris filix-mas	Male fern
Filipendula spp.	Meadowsweet

tain one part garden soil or even clayey loam, one part sand, and one to two parts humus in the form of leaf mold, compost, thoroughly rotted cow manure or sphagnum peat moss. This mixture will be somewhat acidic, but most plants of the shade like it that way. Cover surfaces with mulch.

The woodland plants need this highly moisture-retentive medium that is also very well draining. For efficiency and convenience, also plan for automated irrigation in the planting beds. Consider installing soaker hoses buried within every new bed you make.

For many of us gardeners, shade equals a woodlandlike setting and forest-understory plants. On the other hand, location and scale influence choices as well. Town gardens are often most successful when they have a formal design with paved areas, paths and symmetrical beds that utilize space effectively. This apparent dichotomy can be an exciting design challenge or daunting. Try to blend the formal with the informal. You might make a rectangular reflecting pool to capture the light and bring it down to the garden. Or, perhaps,

Galax urceolata	Galax*
x *Heucherella*	Heucherella
Hosta spp. and hybrids	Hosta, plantain lily*
Houttuynia cordata	Houttuynia (Zone 6-10)
Hylomecon japonicum	Hylomecon
Impatiens walleriana	Impatiens, busy-lizzy (tender perennial)
Lamiastrum galeobdolon	'Herman's Pride', yellow archangel
Ligularia spp.	Ligularia
Liriope spp.	Lily turf*
Lobelia cardinalis	Cardinal flower
Lysimachia nummularia	Creeping jenny
Macleaya cordata	Plume poppy
Maianthemum canadense	False lily-of-the-valley
Osmunda regalis	Royal fern
Ophiopogon spp.	Mondo grass*
Phlox stolonifera	Creeping phlox
Polemonium spp.	Jacob's ladder
Polygonatum spp.	Solomon's seal
Polystichum acrostichoides	Christmas fern
Primula japonica	Japanese primrose
Pulmonaria spp.	Lungwort
Sanguinaria canadensis	Bloodroot
Saxifraga spp.	Saxifrage, strawberry begonia
Smilacina racemosa	False Solomon's seal
Stylophorum diphyllum	Celandine poppy*
Tellima grandiflora	False alumroot
Thalictrum aquilegifolium	Meadow rue
Trachystemon orientalis	Trachystemon
Trollius spp.	Globeflower
Uvularia grandiflora	Great merrybells, bellwort*

create organized beds filled with shade-tolerant woodlanders, edged not by carefully trimmed sun-loving herbs, but by clipped Japanese holly (*Ilex crenata*) or a curb of granite blocks or bricks. The formal garden in the shade could have flowering annuals in its symmetrical beds. The back of the yard and areas for screening along the sides could be home to more naturalistic plantings.

These informal arrangements can be blendings of shrubs and herbaceous perennials such as ferns and hostas, along with native woodlanders. Learn from the model of the forest's tri-leveled hierarchy. Above is the tree-top canopy, which for you might be buildings or your single ornamental tree. The flowering forest understory of shrubs is similar to your garden's layer of woody, shade-tolerant plants. Around these plants that help define the structure or "bones" of the garden, are the next-lower plants, the herbaceous perennials.

Wildflowers will grow along with the cultivated herbaceous species, woody plants and bulbs. Native plants often do

SHADE-TOLERANT SHRUBS

Abelia x *grandiflora*	Glossy abelia (semievergreen)
Acer palmatum	Cut leaf maple*
Aralia elata	Devil's walking stick, angelica tree
Aucuba japonica	Aucuba*
Azalea	see Rhododendron
Berberis spp.	Barberry species
Calycanthus floridus	Sweetshrub*
Camellia japonica	Camellia
Cephalotaxus spp.	Plum-yew
Clethra alnifolia	Sweet pepperbush
Cornus alba (*C. alba* 'Sibirica')	Red-twig dogwood, Tartarian dogwood
Corylopsis spp.	Winter hazel
Daphne x *burkwoodii*	Burkwood daphne
Enkianthus campanulatus	Enkianthus
Euonymus japonicus	Japanese euonymus
E. fortunei radicans	Wintercreeper*
x *Fatshedera lizei*	Tree-ivy
Fatsia japonica	Japanese fatsia
Fothergilla major	Large fothergilla
Gaultheria forestii	Gaultheria
Hamamelis mollis	Chinese witch-hazel
H. virginiana	American witch-hazel
Hibiscus syriacus	Rose-of-Sharon

well because they come from similar locations. The forest floor features a plethora of wildflowers blooming in spring above a blanket of rich-brown mulch (leaves in nature). Select natural-looking organic mulches such as chopped leaves, licorice root, buckwheat hulls or shredded fir bark — avoid large-scale bark chips or quarried gravel. In a small area, more has to be packed into less space, so consider living "mulches" — the ground covers. Ground covers underplanting our horticultural assemblage provide additional chances to collect and grow brilliant miniature specimens, such as false lily-of-the-valley (*Maianthemum canadense*).

The tried-and-true covers for shade may not be as unfamiliar, but are dependable and nearly indestructible. Ivy (*Hedera helix* and many of its cultivars), *Vinca minor* and pachysandra are the top three. Mention pachysandra to most people and they think, "shiny, plastic, pea-green'" — the cover that seems over-used throughout suburban America. There are reasons this Japanese plant is so widely planted. It is easy to grow, adaptable to dense shade and has very low maintenance requirements since it smothers nearly all weeds once it becomes established. There are also new varieties coming along that have interesting serrated and even oak-shaped leaves, and there is a variegated cultivar which, unfortunately, does not spread as rapidly, and the magnificent native species. Although it is also slow-growing, Allegheny

Hydrangea arborescens 'Annabelle'	Tree hydrangea, smooth hydrangea
H. aspera	Rough-leaved hydrangea*
H. quercifolia	Oak-leafed hydrangea*
Ilex spp.	Holly
Itea virginica	Virginia sweetspire
Kalmia latifolia	Mountain laurel
Kerria japonica	Kerria
Leucothoe fontanesiana	Drooping leucothoe
Ligustrum spp.	Privet
Magnolia tomentosa (M.stellata)	Star magnolia
Mahonia japonica	Mahonia
Osmanthus spp.	Tea olive, osmanthus
Pieris spp.	Andromeda
Pittosporum spp.	Pittosporum
Rhododendron spp.	Rhododendron, rosebay
Rhus spp.	Sumac
Salix spp.	Shrub willows
Sarcococca spp.	Sarcococca, sweet box
Skimmia japonica	Japanese skimmia*
Symphoricarpos albus	Snowberry
Taxus spp.	Yew*
Viburnum spp.	Viburnum
Xanthorhiza simplicissima	Yellow root

*Tolerates low light in my garden

spurge (*Pachysandra procumbens*), has beautiful mottled leaves in spring that become solid, matte green by summer. And none of these plants needs to be mowed.

Lawn is not a good choice. Grass needs sun, and even if you have enough light, no living ground cover can take the constant traffic of limited space in the small city garden. Many people insist on lawn, if only to gaze upon, but remember, this tiny swath will have to be mowed, too, and the mower will have to be stored. It may not be worth the trouble to have a green patch that might best be clipped with cuticle scissors. Hard-surface paving materials are best in high-traffic areas, and require less maintenance — only occasional sweeping or hosing.

The list of shade plants is potentially enormous. Open your eyes and mind, see all you can and experiment. You will no doubt try hybrid tea roses once or twice and watch them languish — and finally die, spindly cane by cane. But then one of the tenets of our favorite pastime is "if at first you don't succeed, you're bound to be a gardener."

All of these plants enjoy a bit of sun; however some, especially the woodland wildflowers, will thrive as long as there is bright light. The taller herbaceous perennials that bloom in summer do want as much sun as the shade gardener has — in any event, they will probably require staking to stand tall in the sheltered garden. You may just allow them to flop on top of their neighbors, as I often do.

COLOR ME QUICK

BY TED MARSTON

The French have a phrase for it, "Le sauce c'est tout." When you're cooking up a garden, the annuals are the spice, the sauce, the color. They're the frosting on the cake, the extra zest that makes a lived-in garden come alive. And they're ever so speedy.

This need for quick color is intensified in small town and city spaces where there's no room for grand herbaceous borders. Flower color from trees and shrubs can be dramatic, but their limited number makes them an exuberant splash for only a short time.

In most American climates, annuals provide bright colors and contrasts in textures from early spring through late autumn. And lucky are those in the favored places where color from annuals is enjoyed year-round.

Strictly speaking, annuals are plants which sprout, bloom, set seed and die all in the same year (leaving their progeny to carry on the race next year). But in the small garden, it's best to think of annuals as color spots interwoven in the backbone of the garden for enjoyment this year, and then replanted again the next. This gives you the freedom to use any plant or plant combination for seasonal color.

And actually, many plants we traditionally think of as annuals (such as petunias, snapdragons and bedding geraniums) are really tender perennials, which means they are not winter hardy in most gardens. Biennials, too, which make clumps of leaves the first season, then bloom the second, can be treated as annuals and planted out the spring of the year they bloom.

A barrel overflowing with pink petunias, ivy geraniums, lobelia and other flowers can provide a splash of color in even the tiniest garden.

Such free-spirited thinking widens your plant selection immensely. Many tropical foliage plants, for example, lend golds, purples and bronzes and white-marked green leaves to the summer color scheme. Cordylines are used so often to anchor a tub of geraniums, some think they've become a cliche. But there are a host of of others which also grow vigorously in hot weather such as Swedish ivy or its smaller-leaved, variegated or purple cousins. There's the royal purple of *Setcreasea purpurea,* or the striped leaves of Moses-in-a-Boat *(Rhoeo spathacea).* Dramatically colored foliage plants are perhaps most effective massed in strips or ribbons but can be equally appealing with flowering plants in a mixed container planting.

Tender sub-shrubs such as silvery *Helichrysum petiolatum* and 'Limelight', its

A lushly planted hanging basket enlivens a wooden fence.

ANNUALS FOR BRIGHT SHADE

Impatiens *(Impatiens walleriana)* — 'Accent Hybrids', 'Super Elfin Hybrids', 'Tempo Hybrids'

Tuberous begonia *(Begonia tuberhybrida)* — 'Non-Stop Hybrids', 'Clips Hybrids'

Fibrous begonia *(Begonia semperflorens)* — 'Cocktail Hybrids', 'Varsity Hybrids', 'Prelude Hybrids'

Nicotiana *(Nicotiana alata)* — 'Domino Hybrids', 'Nicki Hybrids'

Browallia *(Browallia speciosa)* — 'Bells Hybrids'

Ageratum *(Ageratum houstonianum)* — 'Blue Danube', 'Hawaii'

Coleus *(Coleus* x *hybridus)* — 'Wizard Hybrids', 'Poncho Hybrids', 'Fiji Hybrids'

Dusty miller *(Senecio bicolor cineraria)* — 'Silver Dust' and 'Silver Lace'

Forget-me-not — *(Myosotis sylvatica)*

Fuchsia *(Fuchsia hybrida)* — 'Swingtime', 'Lena', 'Indian Maid', 'Gartenmeister Bonstedt'

Lobelia *(Lobelia erinus)* — 'Color Cascade Hybrids', 'Cambridge Blue', 'Crystal Palace', 'Sapphire'

Salvia splendens — 'Carabiniere Hybrids', 'Laser Hybrids'

Salvia farinacea — 'Victoria'

Sweet alyssum *(Lobularia maritima)* — 'Wonderland Hybrids'

In addition to coleus, a variety of other foliage plants will work well in the shade, including English ivy *(Hedera helix)*, *Plectranthus* species and variegated ground ivy *(Glecoma hederacea variegata)*. Keep in mind, however, that ground ivy is invasive; use it in containers only.

ANNUALS FOR SUN

Geranium — Zonal geranium *(Pelargonium* x *hortorum)*

    Cutting: 'Tango', 'Forever Yours', 'Blue', 'Snowmass'

    Seed: 'Orbit Hybrids', 'Ringo Hybrids', 'Elite Hybrids'

Ivy geranium *(Pelargonium peltatum)* — Cascade series: 'Galilee', 'Salmon Queen', 'Beauty of Eastbourne'

Petunia *(Petunia* hybrids*)* — 'Ultra Hybrids', 'Super Cascade Hybrids', 'Falcon Hybrids', 'Madness Hybrids', 'Celebrity Hybrids', 'Carpet Hybrids'

French marigold — *(Tagetes patula)* 'Aurora Hybrids', 'Boy Hybrids', 'Bonanza Hybrids', 'Hero Hybrids', 'Disco Hybrids'

Aztec marigold *(Tagetes erecta)* — 'Inca Hybrids', 'Perfection Hybrids', 'Voyager Hybrids' and 'Discovery Hybrids'

Fibrous begonia *(Begonia semperflorens)* — 'Prelude Hybrids', 'Varsity Hybrids'

Pansy *(Viola* x *wittrockiana)* — 'Crystal Bowl Hybrids', 'Universal Hybrids', 'Maxim Hybrids'

Periwinkle *(Catharanthus roseus)* — 'Pretty Hybrids', 'Magic Carpet Hybrids'

Sweet alyssum *(Lobularia maritima)* — 'Wonderland Hybrids'

Salvia *(Salvia farinacea)* — 'Victoria'; *(Salvia splendens)* — 'Carabiniere Hybrids', 'Laser Purple'

Dusty miller *(Senecio bicolor cineraria)* — 'Silver Dust' and 'Silver Lace'

Dianthus *(Dianthus chinensis)* — 'Telstar Hybrids', 'Princess Hybrids'

A terrace provides a perfect setting for a collection of plants in pots, including snapdragons, coleus and a rhododendron.

chartreuse-leafed form, add immense character to the garden as they weave their way through other plants. And ornamental grasses (many of them annual) rustle seductively in summer breezes and are topped by distinctive seed heads in fall that remain decorative all winter.

Good garden centers and nurseries abound with ideas for plants to color your garden. And some, like the ivies, with unusual lobed or feathered leaves or patterns of golds and white are not even found in the annuals section. There are also a wealth of annuals not even found in garden centers. Some are easy and colorful but have difficult names like *Nolana, Venidium* and *Dimorphotheca*. These are the plants you have to

PLANTS FOR FALL & WINTER

Pansy *(Viola* x *wittrockiana)* — 'Universal Hybrids', 'Crystal Bowl Hybrids', 'Maxim Hybrids'

Chrysanthemums (most are not reliably winter hardy)

Ornamental kale & cabbage *(Brassica oleracea)* — 'Dynasty', 'Chidori', 'Peacock'

Primrose *(Primula* vulgaris) — 'Festive Hybrids', 'Ducat Hybrids', 'Julian Hybrids' start yourself from seeds purchased by mail.

While many annuals perform brilliantly from direct seeding in the garden, (*Cosmos* and *Cleome,* for example), others must be started early indoors. Many fine plants can also be started from cuttings: daisies such as marguerites *(Chrysanthemum frutescens)*, for example, or *Verbena* 'Silver Anne' and 'Sissinghurst'.

But it's no secret that much of the action in annuals is at garden centers. There customers find instant color, and various sized plants in small cell packs, six-inch pots and sometimes even larger sizes.

Although some town and city gardens aren't blessed with as much sunlight as their owners would like, a few annuals will give respectable flower display with minimal sun so long as there's bright reflected light to trigger bloom. As the hours of sunlight expand, so too will your choice of plants. And this includes varieties which revel in full sun, as well as those that can thrive in reflected heat from south- or west-facing buildings.

If you're uncertain about the fertility of your soil but don't want to take time to feed regularly, simply add a slow-release fertilizer to your ground beds and containers before planting. Regular watering is also a must for shallow-rooted annuals in ground beds, and even more critical for container plantings.

When space is at a premium, tidiness is next to godliness. Many annuals, such as impatiens, are naturally self-cleaning, since the spent flowers just drop away. Others, such as geraniums grown from seed, must have their spent flower heads removed. Shear back petunias when they grow long and straggly and you'll have copious bloom

Morning glory *(Ipomoea nil, I. purpurea, I. tricolor)* — 'Heavenly Blue Improved', 'Pearly Gates'

Nasturtium *(Tropaeolum majus)* — 'Dwarf Double Jewel', 'Double Gleam Hybrids'

Moss rose *(Portulaca grandiflora)* — 'Sundance Hybrids', 'Sundial Hybrids'

Snapdragon *(Antirrhinum majus)* — 'Rocket Hybrids', 'Princess Hybrids','Floral Carpet Hybrids'

Sweet Pea *(Lathyrus odoratus)* — many varieties

Verbena *(Verbena* x *hybrida)* — 'Romance Hybrids', 'Springtime Hybrids'

Zinnia *(Zinnia elegans)* — 'Zenith Hybrids', 'Peter Pan Hybrids', 'Border Beauty Hybrids'

Hollyhock *(Alcea rosea)* — 'Powderpuff Hybrids', 'Majorette Hybrids', 'Summer Carnival'

Cosmos *(Cosmos bipinnatus)* — 'Sensation', 'Seashells'

(Cosmos sulphureus) — 'Sunny Hybrids'

Globe amaranth *(Gomphrena globosa)* — 'Buddy', 'Strawberry Fields'

Blue marguerite *(Felicia amelloides)*

Chilean bell flower *(Nolana paradoxa)* — 'Blue Bird'

Corn cockle *(Agrostemma githago)* — 'Milas Cerise'

African daisy (*Arctotis stoechadifolia*)

Dahlberg daisy (*Dyssodia tenuiloba*)

Swan River daisy *(Brachycome iberidifolia)* — Splendor series

Gazania *(Gazania rigens)* — 'Daybreak Hybrids', 'Chansonette Hybrids'

Godetia *(Clarkia amoena)* — 'Grace Hybrids'

Prairie gentian *(Eustoma grandiflorum)* — 'Yodel Hybrids', 'Lion Hybrids'

Cape marigold (*Dimorphotheca* hybrids) — 'Starshine', 'Tetra Pole Star'

Melampodium *(Melampodium paludosum)* — 'Medallion'

Monkey flower *(Mimulus hybridus)* — 'Calypso Hybrids', 'Malibu Hybrids'

Nemesia *(Nemesia strumosa)* — 'Carnival Hybrids', 'Tapestry'

Nierembergia (*Nierembergia hippomanica violacea*) — 'Purple Robe'

Iceland poppy *(Papaver nudicaule)* — 'Wonderland Hybrids', 'Oregon Rainbows'

Primrose (*Primula vulgaris*) — 'Festive', 'Pacific Giant'

Butterfly flower (*Schizanthus* x *wisetonensis*)

African daisy (*Arctotis fastuosa*) — 'Zulu Prince'

Wallflower (*Cheiranthus cheiri*) — 'Blood Red', 'Cloth of Gold'

on compact plants again.

The hues you choose for planting should be your favorites. Consider the purity of white in the garden as a leavener of stronger colors, and for its nighttime ambience as it sparkles in the lights of a deck or terrace. Remember, too, that dark flowers recede, while bright flowers intrude. And several plants of one color are usually better than a variety of annuals of many different hues.

But don't let your head be turned only by flower color. Remember to look too at the plant's foliage textures.

PERENNIALS FOR TOWN & CITY GARDENS

BY RUTH ROGERS CLAUSEN

&

NICOLAS H. EKSTROM

own and city gardens, small by definition, are intimate spaces important in relieving the harshness of the urban landscape. Their limited size is far outweighed by the extent to which they improve the quality of life.

While smallness of space may be an advantage in terms of labor, it presents certain inherent problems in garden design. Privacy is a critical factor due to the closeness of neighbors, but trees and shrubs, hedges and even fences can supply necessary screening, while making an ideal setting for smaller plants and perennials. Background plantings, as well as attention to scale in the selection of perennials, can provide an illusion of space.

In small town and city gardens, which are enjoyed throughout the year, shrubs are often combined with perennials to furnish off-season interest. Some perennials, regrettably few in number, retain their foliage throughout the winter; some of our

favorites in our New York gardens include variegated lily-turf (*Liriope muscari* 'Variegata'), many of the coral bells (*Heuchera*), European ginger (*Asarum europaeum*), strawberry begonia (*Saxifraga stolonifera*) and evergreen ferns such as Christmas fern (*Polystichum acrostichoides*). The dry foliage and elegant fruiting heads of ornamental grasses also remain attractive for most of the winter months.

Less costly than shrubs, more permanent than annuals, perennials cover a broad and varied range. Even the novice can achieve a sophisticated complexity of design by using a variety of these plants.

The choice of flower color is a personal one, but it's well to remember that cool colors such as blues and whites create an illusion of distance, whereas strong hot colors create the opposite effect.

The season of bloom for most perennials is fleeting, so it is particularly important in a small garden to select plants with what

Astilbe, left center, and yarrow, lower right, are among the perennials recommended for city gardens.

is known as "good foliage." This term implies not only that the leaves are durable, but that the plant has an attractive habit as well as foliage that is interesting in shape, texture or color.

Certain practical problems are associated with urban gardening. There is shade, for example, which not only limits the selection of usable plants, but from a design standpoint must be brightened with white or light-colored flowers or variegated foliage. Unfortunately, few silver- and gray-leaved plants thrive in minimal sunlight.

Due to the proximity of buildings and other structures, an urban garden may suffer from poor drainage. The soil may be compacted from heavy use and is frequently exhausted since organic materials are not naturally renewed each year. So amending and fertilizing the soil is of prime importance. Raised beds, as well as containers, may be employed so that the quality of the soil can be readily controlled. Moreover, raised beds create a variation in height, providing interest in limited spaces.

The plants in town and city gardens must be chosen for tolerance of both pollution and the heat retained by the hardscape.

In confined spaces, pest and disease problems are aggravated, and it is important to control them quickly, since the damage is especially noticeable close up.

The following short list of perennials includes many that we grow in our own gardens. We have chosen them with availability and ease of culture in mind.

The following abbreviations are used in the plant list: SP=spring, SU=summer, F=fall, E=early and L=late. The letters H and T following the zones of hardiness indicate, respectively, the sensitivity to or tolerance of combined heat and humidity in our hottest zones.

LATIN NAME	COMMON NAME

Achillea 'Moonshine' — **Yarrow**
Its pale lemon yellow flowers and gray foliage combine beautifully with *Salvia* x *superba*

Anemone x hybrida — **Japanese anemone**
White 'Honorine Jobert' is an elegant old cultivar.

Artemisia 'Powis Castle' — _____
The only *Artemisia* to hold up well during the dog days of August.

Aruncus dioicus — **Goatsbeard**
Resembles a giant white Astilbe.

Asarum europaeum — **European wild ginger**
Without a doubt, one of the most elegant of evergreen ground covers.

Aster x frikartii — _____
A non-stop bloomer! 'Wonder of Staffa' is a good form.

Astilbe x arendsii — _____
Many cultivars in white, pink and red.

Brunnera macrophylla — **Siberian bugloss**
Airy sprays of intense blue forget-me-not flowers.

Ceratostigma plumbaginoides — **Leadwort**
An excellent late-blooming ground cover.

Chrysanthemum nipponicum — **Nippon daisy**
Extremely tolerant of seaside conditions.

Cimicifuga racemosa — **Bugbane**
Tall spires of white flowers above excellent divided foliage.

Chrysogonum virginianum — **Goldenstar**
A useful, long-blooming ground cover around shrubs.

Coreopsis verticillata — **Thread-leaf coreopsis**
Flowers profusely over a long season. 'Moonbeam' has pale yellow flowers.

Corydalis lutea — _____
Try growing it in walls and between paving stones.

Dicentra eximia — **Fringed bleeding-heart**
Its ferny foliage persists all summer, unlike that of *Dicentra spectabilis*.

Echinacea purpurea — **Purple coneflower**
A difficult purplish-pink to combine with other colors.

Epimedium grandiflorum — **Longspur epimedium**
Look for the white-flowered form. Good in dry shade.

Erigeron x hybridus — **Fleabane**
Many cultivars in pink to violet and purple.

Eryngium bourgatii — _____
Once a collector's plant, but now quite generally available.

Euphorbia polychroma — **Cushion spurge**
The neat mound of foliage turns red in the fall.

Color	Bloom Time	Height	Sun/Shade	Zones
yellow	SU	2'	◎	10-3/T
pink	LSU-F	3'-5'	◎ ◉	10-6
——	——	2'-3'	◎	10-5/H
white	SU	4'-6'	◎ ◉	9-3
brown	SP	6"	◉ ●	8-4
lavender	ESU-F	2'-3'	◎ ◉	10-5/H
various	ESU-SU	2'-3.5'	◎ ◉	8-4
blue	LSP	1.5'	◎ ◉	10-3/H
blue	LSU/F	1'	◎ ◉	10-5
white	F	1.5'-3'	◎	10-5/T
white	SU	4'-6'	◎ ◉	10-3/H
yellow	SP-F	4"-1'	◎ ◉	10-5/T
yellow	SU-F	1'-3'	◎	10-3/T
yellow	SP-F	12"-15"	◎ ◉	10-5/H
pink	SP-SU	1'-1.5'	◉ ●	10-3/H
purple	SU	2'-4'	◎	10-3/T
red	SP	1'-1.5'	◉ ●	8-4
various	SP-F	1'-2.5'	◎	10-6
green	SU	1'-1.5'	◎	10-5
yellow	SP/LSP	1.5'-2'	◎ ◉	9-3

LATIN NAME	COMMON NAME
Gaillardia x *grandiflora* Easy-to-grow and drought-tolerant.	**Blanket flower**
Galium odoratum A bright ground cover with dainty whorled leaves.	**Sweet woodruff**
Geranium x oxonianum **'Claridge Druce'** Vigorous and free flowering.	**Hardy geranium**
Geranium sanguineum **var.** *striatum* A very well-behaved little plant.	**Hardy geranium**
Helleborus orientalis The hybrids range in color from pale green and white to pink and maroon.	**Lenten rose**
Heuchera x *brizoides* Red, pink or more rarely white flowers above evergreen foliage.	**Coral bells**
Hosta plantaginea Very fragrant, pure white trumpets high above the foliage.	**August lily**
Kirengeshoma palmata Often blooms right up to the first frost.	————
Liriope muscari Late-season flower spikes are followed by pretty, shiny black fruits.	**Big blue lilyturf**
Lysimachia punctata Invasive, like most of the loosestrifes.	**Yellow loosestrife**
Myrrhis odorata The dark brown, ribbed seeds are even more ornamental than the tiny white flowers.	**Sweet cicely**
Physostegia virginiana 'Summer Snow' is a popular cultivar with pure white flowers.	**False dragonhead**
Pulmonaria saccharata 'Mrs. Moon' has leaves well marked with large, silvery spots.	**Bethlehem sage**
Salvia x *superba* All the cultivars of this sage are indispensable plants for the sunny garden.	**Purple sage**
Saxifraga stolonifera This familiar houseplant is surprisingly hardy out of doors.	**Strawberry begonia**
Sempervivum tectorum Best grown in rock gardens, walls or containers.	**Hen-and-chickens**
Sidalcea malviflora Several fine cultivars are available in a range of pinks.	**Prairie mallow**
Thalictrum rochebrunianum Truly a distinguished and elegant plant.	**Meadow rue**
Tiarella cordifolia A charming native for shaded gardens.	**Foamflower**
Tricyrtis hirta White orchidlike flowers spotted and speckled with dark purple.	**Hairy toad-lily**

COLOR	BLOOM TIME	HEIGHT	SUN/SHADE	ZONES
various	ESU-F	2'-3'	◎	10-3/H
white	LSP	6"-1'	◉	9-3/H
pink	ESU-EF	1.5'-2'	◎ ◉	9-4/H
pink	LSP-SU	1'	◎ ◉	10-4/H
various	ESP	1.5'-2'	◉ ●	10-3/H
various	SP-SU	1.5'-2.5'	◎ ◉	10-3
white	SU	2'	◉ ●	9-3
yellow	LSU/EF	3'-4'	◉	9-5
purple	F	1'-1.5'	◎ ●	10-5/T
yellow	SU	1.5'-2.5'	◎ ◉	9-4
white	ESU	3'-4'	◎ ◉	9-4
pink	SU-F	2'-3'	◎ ◉	10-3/H
blue	SP	1'-1.5'	◉ ●	9-3
purple	LSP-LSU	1.5'-3'	◎	10-5
white	LSP	1'-2'	◉ ●	10-6/H
pink	SU	1'-1.5'	◎	10-5
pink	SU	2'-4'	◎ ◉	10-5
purple	SU/EF	4'-6'	◎ ◉	10-5/H
white	LSP/ESU	1'	◉	9-3
white	EF-LF	1'-3'	◉ ●	9-5

GOOD HEDGES
FOR GOOD NEIGHBORS &
OTHER GARDEN USES

BY LINDA YANG

Good hedges make good neighbors — maybe even better than fences (with apologies to Robert Frost). Hedgerows were used in the Middle Ages to define property and contain animals. But in the modern town, hedges provide the privacy that helps ensure sanity. A hedge is, after all, a polite screen for neighbors and passersby.

Clipped or unclipped, a hedge also tempers the wind, muffles the sound of traffic, provides elegant cover for unsightly views and a fine backdrop for flowers.

Whatever the season, it's never too late to start a hedge. If you're a yard gardener, prepare for planting by digging a trench or a straight line of holes, using a hose as a linear guide. If you're a rooftop gardener, begin with several containers that are at least 18 inches deep and wide, and are filled with a blend of equal parts topsoil, perlite and peat moss.

For each plant, stir in a shovelful of cow manure and a handful of a granular 5-10-5 fertilizer. After planting, add a mulch of bark chips and keep the area well watered. Leave a shallow depression around the base of each plant so that moisture collects.

The spacing between the plants will depend on the rate of growth and ultimate size of the varieties you've chosen. The farther apart, the longer it takes for the hedge shape to form. In general, the space between should be somewhat less than the plant's mature width. Rooftop plants and those to be sheared as formal hedges can be closer. Unsheared or informal hedge plants can be given a bit more room. Stagger species that are to be windbreaks or place them in multiple rows.

It will be more expensive, but it is best to use container-grown or balled and

A hedge of junipers and arbovitaes planted in containers makes a strong architectural statement in this terrace garden.

A clipped boxwood hedge flanking a white wooden bench
makes a formal statement.

burlaped plants for your hedge. In addition to providing instant gratification, container-grown plants are less likely to die, easier to plant and are often quite well branched. But more importantly, they don't need the severe pruning that bare-root plants must have at planting time to compensate for the root loss and encourage a dense twig mass.

Container plants need only be lightly sheared the first summer to encourage density. The following spring, deciduous plants and broadleaved evergreens should be more drastically clipped to force new growth and multiple branching, and to make the mass uniform. Needle evergreens should be lightly sheared except for yews, which may need some trimming again in summer.

If you've started with very young plants, shear them once they begin to grow noticeably. Until they achieve full size, the shoots of the previous year's growth can be reduced by about one third. Or, as one nurseryman once put it, "If you want to have a tall tight hedge, you must first develop a small tight hedge — and then let it grow, gradually. Don't wait until it gets to the height you want before you start shaping it."

If a formally clipped hedge is your goal, don't trust your eye; use temporary stakes at each end and run a taut string as your guide. To keep the top branches from

HEDGE PLANTS THAT DO BEST WITH AT LEAST SEVEN HOURS OF SUN

....

Arborvitae (*Thuja occidentalis*)

Barberry (*Berberis thunbergii*)

Corkscrew willow (*Salix matsudana* 'Tortuosa')

False cypress (*Chamaecyparis pisifera)*

Hornbeam (*Carpinus caroliniana*)

Juniper 'Skyrocket' (*Juniperus virginiana* 'Skyrocket')

Lilac (*Syringa* spp.)

Autumn olive (*Eleagnus angustifolia*)

Trifoliate orange (*Poncirus trifoliata*)

HEDGE PLANTS THAT TOLERATE A MINIMUM OF FOUR HOURS OF SUN

....

Bamboo *(Phyllostachys* spp.)

Crabapple (*Malus* spp.)

Firethorn (*Pyracantha coccinea*)

Forsythia (*Forsythia* spp.)

Hedge cotoneaster (*Cotoneaster lucidus*)

Hemlock (*Tsuga canadensis*)

Holly (*Ilex* spp.)

Inkberry (*Ilex glabra*)

Peegee hydrangea (*Hydrangea paniculata* 'Grandiflora')

Privet (*Ligustrum vulgare*)

Rose-of-Sharon (*Hibiscus syriacus*)

Rhododendron (*Rhododendron* spp.)

Winged spindle bush (*Euonymus alatus*)

Yew (*Taxus baccata*)

shading those on the bottom, slope each side slightly to create a somewhat wider base. A rounded top also reduces injury from the weight of piled-up snow.

Flowering species can be used as a decorative screen. Prune early spring bloomers right after they flower. Prune summer bloomers in spring or winter. Remember that even informal hedges need care to keep them from degenerating from casual to careless.

And finally, be sure to place your hedge on your side of the property line. As the plants mature and spread, a cantankerous neighbor has the right — legitimately — to chop off any intruders.

Hedge Plants For City Gardens

Many trees and shrubs can be used for hedges. Whether they're grown in containers or in the ground, plants for hedges are best chosen with a specific purpose in mind. A hedge planned to discourage trespassers might include thorny species like hardy orange or roses. An informal divider that's primarily decorative might be developed from flowering shrubs like forsythia or rose-of-Sharon. For a formal design use plants amenable to repeated clipping, like Japanese holly or yew. And if you want to mix and match (as the British do), use plants with a similar rate of growth and equal tolerance of shearing.

Adapted from "Green Screen: The Hedge's Polite Rebuff" by Linda Yang, which first appeared in The New York Times *in August 1989.*

31

URBANE WILDFLOWERS

BY PATTI HAGAN

City gardeners garden defensively, or not at all. But due to the difference between street culture and backyard culture, a good front-line defense is not at all the same as a good back-line defense.

Out front, city gardeners fight the elements: natural, unnatural and human. The exposed position, whether sunny or shady, tends to aridity. The exposed position also tends to encourage fast-flower, self-service blossom and plant thieves. Out back, city gardeners must defend against shade — the implacable shade of buildings and the insidious, creeping shade of leafing trees that by late spring obliterates many early spring sunspots.

In both garden cultures a new ecological succession is happening. The typical city front-yard story begins when, the first spring on the block, the green urban gardener puts out a normal suburban spread, say, ageratum, marigolds, pinks, geraniums, hybrid petunias, and almost immediately the plants go AWOL. They are uplifted, uprooted: they walk. Several re-installments later existential frontyard despair sets in: the beginning of frontyard wisdom.

For weeds and wildflowers are opportunists that abhor a vacuum. They will finish out the season for the gardener.

Next year, next stage. By this time the gardener may have staked out some vacant lots — reduced to first generation rubble — and may have noticed, among the shards of brick and mortar, rugged stands of wildflowers. The gardener may even have done some casual deadheading, dried the wild finds, turned the soil out front, and turned the seeds in for winter. After several years such a gardener has not a front yard, but a front meadow: doily-white overstory of Queen Anne's lace, embroidered with Deptford pink, chicory, moth mullein, sunflowers, butter-and-eggs, cinquefoil, spotted knapweed, clover, *Monarda*, butterfly-weed, *Centaurea,* fleabane, asters, wild sweet pea, the black-eyed Susans, evening primrose, *Thermopsis caroliniana, Liatris* and wild petunia with grasses. Rather than continue imperialistically to try to impose formal European gardening conventions on an intractable city site, the gardener has gone native.

The urban wildflower front meadow is

32

Handsome by day, Queen Anne's lace is a standout in the sodium-vapor dark of the urban night meadow.

sufficient unto itself. It takes little tending, but rewards attention. The meadow plants are so tough and grow so well *unencouraged* that any slight encouragement, such as compost or manure, causes them to grow wildly. In addition, this garden is almost impervious to drought.

Even better, since these flowers lack florist equivalents, they have no street value. If they're called anything by local passersby, they're called weeds. And on the street weeds are worthless. Flower snitches pass them by. Furthermore, Queen Anne's lace, evening primrose and black-eyed Susan are great city nightflowers, standouts in the sodium-vapor-dark of the urban night meadow.

In addition, the wildflower meadow can be extended along a street demimeadow fashion. Planted in street tree pits, these sturdy flowers can sometimes gain enough presence to discourage dogs and dog-owners from misusing the T-pits for latrines.

Bluestone Perennials
7211 Middle Ridge Road
Madison, OH 44057
800-852-5243

Canyon Creek Nursery
3527 Dry Creek Road
Oroville, CA 95965
916-533-2166
Catalog, $1

Crownsville Nursery
P.O. Box 797
Crownsville, MD 21032
301-923-2212
Catalog, $2

Eastern Plant Specialties
Box 226
Georgetown, ME 04548
207-371-2888
Catalog, $2

Forestfarm
990 Tetherow Road
Williams, OR 97544-9599
Catalog, $3

J.L. Hudson, Seedsman
P.O. Box 1058
Redwood City, CA 94064
Catalog, $1

Heronswood Nursery
7530 288th Street NE
Kingston, WA 98346
206-297-4172
Catalog, $3

High Altitude Gardens
Box 4619 • Ketchum ID 83340
800-874-7333
Catalog, $2

Holbrook Farm
Rt. 2, Box 223B • Fletcher, NC 28732
704-891-7790
Catalog, $2

Montrose Nursery
P.O. Box 957 • Hillsborough, NC 27278
919-732-7787
Catalog, $2

Niche Gardens
1111 Dawson Road • Chapel Hill NC 27516
919-967-0078
Catalog, $3

Peace Seeds
2385 Southeast Thompson St.
Corvallis, OR 97333
Catalog, $5; list, $1

Prairie Nursery
Box 306 • Westfield, WI 53964
608-296-3679
Catalog, $3

Sunlight Gardens
Rte 1, Box 600-A, Hillvale Road
Andersonville, TN 37705
615-494-8237
Catalog, $3

Tripple Brook Farm
37 Middle Road
Southampton MA 01073
413-527-4626

Celandine poppy and foamflower, which tolerate shade, are good candidates for the backyard city garden.

For those lacking the place or the patience to collect seed, most of the major seed houses offer packets of wildflower seed (labeled for region, climate, soil) and certain seedsmen specialize only in wildflowers.

Meantime, in the backyard shadehold, a similar story unfolds. Year one, the gardener attempts to push the shade tolerance of phlox, snapdragons and sunflowers and ends up with a lot of stretched-out, anorexic plants and little bloom. This sort of unflorescence also causes despair. Having lost the first backyard bout to shade, the gardener decides rather than curse the darkness where only mushrooms grow, to plant impatiens. Another year and the gardener curses the impatiens. There is such a thing as a boredom of impatiens.

A walk in the woods, or a visit to the Native Plant Garden of The New York Botanical, or the Local Flora Section of Brooklyn Botanic may implant ideas both

FRESH MEADOW WILDFLOWERS

....

Daylily	*Hemerocallis fulva*
Yarrow	*Achillea*
Queen Anne's lace	*Daucus carota*
Deptford pink	*Dianthus armeria*
Chicory	*Cichorium intybus*
Moth mullein	*Verbascum blattaria*
Sunflower	*Helianthus*
Butter-and-eggs	*Linaria vulgaris*
Cinquefoil	*Potentilla*
Spotted knapweed	*Centaurea maculosa*
Clover	*Trifolium*
Monarda, bee balm	*Monarda fistulosa*
Butterfly-weed	*Asclepias tuberosa*
Centaurea	*Centaurea*
Fleabane	*Erigeron philadelphicus*
Aster	*Aster*
Everlasting pea	*Lathyrus latifolius*
Black-eyed Susan	*Rudbeckia,* esp. *R. triloba*
Evening primrose	*Oenothera biennis*
Thermopsis	*Thermopsis caroliniana*
Liatris	*Liatris*
Wild petunia	*Petunia violacea*
Goldenrod	*Solidago*
Boneset	*Eupatorium perfoliatum*
Joe-Pye-weed	*Eupatorium purpureum*
Compass-plant	*Silphium laciniatum*
Coreopsis	*Coreopsis*

WOODLAND WILDFLOWERS FOR SHADE

....

Foamflower	*Tiarella cordifolia*
Solomon's seal	*Polygonatum biflorum*
Wild geranium	*Geranium maculatum*
Herb-Robert	*Geranium robertianum*
Cimicifuga	*Cimicifuga*
Spring beauty	*Claytonia virginica*
Wood aster	*Aster divaricatus*
Vancouveria	*Vancouveria hexandra*
Houttuynia	*Houttuynia cordata*
Lobelia	*Lobelia cardinalis, L. siphilitica*
Liriope	*Liriope*
Chelone	*Chelone lyoni*
Spiderwort	*Tradescantia virginiana*
Celandine poppy	*Stylophorum diphyllum*
Violet	*Viola*

wild and woodland. Again, the impulse is to go native. Woodland wildlings need the protected, even sheltered backyard environment, where nothing much heavier than a butterfly or bee will ever land on them. Provided they are properly coddled — with leaf mold, humus and moisture — these plants can do well in the city. They can be ordered by mail — but should only be ordered from nurseries that *propagate* the natives they sell. (Caveat emptor! Under Federal Trade Commission nursery guidelines wild-collect-

Queen Anne's lace, black-eyed Susans and other denizens of the urban front meadow take little tending. Even better, because they have no florist equivalents, flower snitches pass them by.

ed plants temporarily parked and "grown in the nursery row for at least one growing season before being marketed" can be sold and advertised as "nursery grown.") Introduce them in spring or fall. Since the flowers tend to be minute, they are best planted in stands of a kind. Over the years they will self-sow and run, eventually massing like true woodland ground covers.

Habitues of woods shade can become quite at home, even comfortable, in city shade. Woods plants to order for a start include foamflower, Solomon's seal, the wild geraniums (cranesbill and herb Robert), *Cimicifuga*, spring beauty, wood aster, *Vancouveria hexandra, Houttuynia*, the lobelias (*L. syphilitica* and *L. cardinalis*), *Liriope, Chelone* and the ferns — Goldie's, cinnamon, ostrich, sensitive, hay-scented, Christmas — to frond the fenceline, not forgetting the violets, perhaps the least shrinking, most aggressive of wildflowers, that will thrive even for those lacking green index fingers. ⋀⋀⋀⋀⋀

FRONT DOOR LANDSCAPES

BY MARY RILEY SMITH

The front yard deserves more attention than it gets. As the setting for a house and as the daily connection to the community, the front property presents design opportunities and challenges of its own. It may be time now to look at your front yard with new eyes. If it's the sunniest part of your property it may be an ideal site for a garden. Even the smallest entry court of a city house offers opportunities for attractive and suitable planting.

Old-Fashioned Front Yards

A look at the traditions of American front yard design may provide ideas for today's front landscapes. In New England enclosed cottage gardens at the front door provided herbs and vegetables for daily use as well as visual pleasure. In the Southwest Spanish influence dictated courtyards enclosed by adobe or stucco walls. Also used in Florida, this style provides a shady and private entrance as well as an outdoor room. Often a fountain is featured and surrounded by plants in pots. And in old neighborhoods of New Orleans and Charleston, entrances are on the side of the house and are arrived at through a gate in a fence

along the sidewalk. These enclosed, self-contained gardens were largely ignored in the late nineteenth and twentieth centuries when more romantic notions of landscaping were popular.

Open Front Yards and Foundation Plantings

Open front yards with little delineation between properties grew out of the nineteenth century interest in natural landscapes. Boundaries and property lines were blurred by loose plantings rather than walls or fences, giving the impression of flowing space. Open properties also seemed more democratic than those shut off from view by fences and gates.

The flowing landscape prevailed even as properties were shrinking in the 1940s and '50s, and in most American towns front yards are usually contiguous or have minimal separation. Along with open front yards, foundation planting is also prevalent. The passion for shrubs set against the base of houses started with the Victorians' large-scale buildings. Shrubs set against these big houses made them appear to be grounded to their sites. In

The front yard is the place to show off your horticultural skills. This gingerbread house is embraced by the carefully clipped specimens.

time, as houses and lots shrank, foundation planting persisted. Shrubs planted along the foundation quickly dwarfed a small house. To keep yews, forsythia and azaleas from blocking windows severe pruning is necessary, creating almost bonsai-like bushes.

Shearing front garden shrubs has also led to a vertical/horizontal/vertical pattern across the facade. Vertical evergreens flank the front door, and lines of clipped shrubs run horizontally under the front windows, ending with vertical shrubs at the corners of the house. The uniformity of these front yard designs could be nicknamed the "American Front Yard Style."

Front Yard Basics

The front yard may be the best place on your property to have a garden, or perhaps show off your horticultural skills while simultaneously perking up the

An informal planting softens the harsh lines of urban buildings.

neighborhood. One of the first things to consider is how the front yard and its plantings set off your house. The landscaping should enhance it — not hide it. A large tree or shrub some distance from the building softens hard architectural lines. The same plant growing against the building distracts from the architecture and makes it seem cramped. Suitability is important, too. Consider the architectural style of the house. If it's Victorian, for instance, bright flowers, urns, a fence and topiary shrubs are appropriate. Simple streamlined plantings are more in keeping with modern architecture.

Function is also important. Does the design adequately meet service needs such as garbage pick-up, car parking and entrance to the house? Is the entry well marked, lighted and welcoming? In older towns and cities where there are rear alleys for garages and garbage pick-up, the front yard may only have a path from the sidewalk to the front door. In this case, a comfortable walk and lighting are of paramount importance.

Carefully clipped evergreen corkscrews echo the strong vertical lines
of the elegant front door.

When deciding on the best use of a front yard, you might begin by addressing the question of the service functions — driveway, parking, garage, garbage pickup and paths. To what extent should they define the front of the property? And if these elements dominate, how might they be minimized or softened?

Garage, Driveway, Parking

Modern houses generally have a garage and driveway facing the sidewalk, on the same plane as the front of the house. Treat-ing them as a single service area can diminish clutter by confining visitor parking, garbage containers, gas tanks and storage to one space. If visitors can park on the street, a driveway will suffice. When visitors must park on your property, a pull-in area next to the driveway might be needed for extra cars. If there is a choice, keeping the driveway to the side of the property enhances a feeling of spaciousness in the front. Likewise, a center path from the sidewalk to the front door can be re-routed to the side.

Diminishing the impact of driveways, cars and other service elements is a worthy goal. A fence or hedge parallel to the driveway can serve as a divider, separating it from the rest of the front property, much like a room divider, reducing its visual impact. A gate through the hedge or fence also creates a psychological passage. Think of the garage and driveway as a work space and the rest of the front as an attractive setting for your house.

Public or Private?

Another major consideration is whether you want the privacy that hedges or fences provide, or openness and curb appeal. Reasons for enclosing the front may be aesthetic or practical. Practical concerns might include keeping children or pets enclosed, planting a windbreak, reducing traffic noise or, simply, having privacy. Aesthetic considerations include creating vertical planes in a flat landscape for variety or as a backdrop for gardens, blocking an unattractive view or easing the transition between the house and driveway or street. In a busy urban area, closing the small space in front of a townhouse creates a psychological transition from the hustle and bustle of the sidewalk. Whether the enclosure is a solid brick wall or a filigree iron fence typical of nineteenth century houses, delineating your property offers psychological privacy, if not actual privacy. But before deciding on a front enclosure, check local zoning rules. Some communities have height restrictions on fences and hedges along sidewalks.

In towns where zoning laws forbid fences or hedges a small enclosure near the front door or along a front path can provide seclusion. Even if turning the front into a garden isn't your goal, a fence, possibly with a gate and arbor, adds distinction.

Assuming you are able to close off the front property, style, cost and function will affect your choice of materials. If the purpose of a front enclosure is privacy, a six-to-eight-foot tall hedge or fence will do the job. A lower enclosure will keep children and pets in or separate the driveway. Walls and fences are more expensive to install than hedges, and most Americans choose hedges or trees to enclose the yard. But don't forget that while a hedge may be less expensive to install, it will require clipping. When considering your front enclosure, be sure to choose a style of fencing or hedging compatible with your home. An informal grape stake fence, for example, is incompatible with a formal brick house. A painted wood fence or an evergreen hedge might be better.

Structures

If you are planning to have a garden in front of the house, consider giving it a framework or backdrop. Although it is possible to create island beds in the front lawn, your design will be improved with such architectural elements as fences, hedges or paths. When designing these structures and choosing plants, don't forget how the garden appears in winter. Tough evergreens, for example, which cheer frosty Northeast and Midwest landscapes, also set off bright perennials and annuals the rest of the year. In the mild-wintered South and West look for plants which play a supporting role for year-round interest, require minimal care and have an elegance that makes them pleasing all year. A bench, sculpture, a sundial or pots and urns provide winter personality, too.

In dense urban areas where townhouses and apartment buildings with little or no garden space are the norm, horticulture plays a vital role. The porch of a brownstone, for example, might be enhanced by planters painted shiny green or black filled with evergreens carefully pruned into architectural shapes. Seasonal interest can be provided by small spring bulbs and bright annuals.

Frequently used entrances can be enlivened with plants. Here, ivy clambers across the steps and climbs up the facade of a brownstone rowhouse.

Such planters can become miniature gardens. An apartment building entry may be enhanced with elegant planters in scale with the facade and filled to overflowing.

Entrances

Cast a critical eye on your most frequently used entrance, no matter if it is the kitchen or front door. It is easy to stop noticing an entrance used several times a day. Would your trips be more pleasant if you were passing through a small herb garden? Pots of topiary herbs on either side of the door not only add charm but are handy for cooking. A fragrant vine on a porch rail or an espaliered pyracantha, orange-berried in winter, make daily trips in and out that much more pleasurable. A large front porch is even more welcoming with a swing or glider, some chairs and pots flanking the door and steps.

Your front yard can be more than a polite landscape. It can be a bright garden for neighbors or an intimate enclosed space for privacy, as well as a charming landscaped picture from inside. ⋀⋀⋀⋀⋀⋀⋀⋀

TAKING CHARGE OF YOUR STREET TREE

BY NINA BASSUK

After you've finished landscaping your windowsill, harvesting the pole beans growing up your fire escape and converting your backyard into an oasis of green, consider taking charge of the tree in front of your house. Yes, in most cities these street trees are owned by the municipality. But in some real way, because you experience their shade and loveliness multiple times a day, they are yours — and they are in trouble.

Consider this: The average lifespan of a tree in a downtown site is just a few years. Only about half the available city planting spaces actually contain trees at any given time. For every tree planted, approximately four are removed. And of every dollar spent on street maintenance and improvements, a mere penny or two goes to trees.

Why are street trees doing poorly?

Below ground the factors affecting tree root growth can be numerous. Deicing salts (NaCl primarily) in North American cities where winter driving conditions are hazardous can do tremendous damage to street trees. High salt levels in the soil decrease the availability of water to the roots, causing a "chemical drought." Moreover, chloride ions are readily taken up by plant roots and can accumulate to toxic levels in the leaves, resulting in marginal leaf necrosis or "scorch." Our analysis of chloride in *Tilia cordata* 'Greenspire' trees growing in New York City showed chloride levels to be 1.8 percent of leaf dry weight, well above acceptable levels. Sodium can also have a detrimental effect on soil structure, leading to increased soil compaction. And salt spray from dissolved road salts can desiccate evergreen leaves directly.

Barriers to root growth resulting in de facto containerization of street trees is also a common occurrence. Utility pipes, asphalt and concrete curbs, rubble in the soil and underground subways and basements, as well as soil compaction, all serve to limit the amount of soil tree roots have

Street trees alongside containers with colorful annuals
soften cityscapes and add charm.

to explore to acquire water and nutrients. Compaction may limit root growth directly by mechanical impedance, or indirectly by reducing soil pore space and thus oxygen diffusion to the root zone. Waterlogged conditions often follow, aggravating damage to root systems due to lack of oxygen.

Urban soil can contain anything from good topsoil to brick rubble and builders' fill. Because many of these materials contain limestone, street tree pit soils are often alkaline, which limits the availability of certain nutrients such as iron and manganese. Pin oak *(Quercus palustris)* is particularly sensitive to high pH soils, resulting in chlorosis.

Urban soils can be extremely variable in fertility and toxic substances as well. "Graywater" is often poured onto street tree pits in a well-meaning attempt at

A mass of impatiens beautifies a street tree pit. Although flowering annuals will compete with tree roots for much needed water and nutrients, they will remind you to water during hot or dry spells.

watering. However, if this spent wash water contains bleach or other toxic chemicals it can be lethal.

Above ground there are still other ways in which the city causes stress in street trees. Foremost among these is reradiated heat from buildings, asphalt, car tops and concrete. The hotter the air temperature around tree canopies, the faster trees lose water and deplete their already limited underground supplies. A study conducted by Cornell's Urban Horticulture Institute in New York City documented that air temperature may be as high as 22 degrees F hotter on the street than the official weather reports indicate.

In certain urban areas, wind also increases leaf desiccation as it speeds up through the "urban canyons" between tall buildings.

Tall buildings, causing false horizons, alter light patterns for many urban trees. Trees on the north side of a city block see far less direct sunlight than those on the east, west or south sides.

Air pollution is often cited as a problem for plant growth in cities; however, this depends very much on the air drainage patterns of a particular location. In New York City it is rare to see symptoms of air pollu-

Marigolds, ivy and elegant wrought-iron edging
help prevent damage by bicycles,
cars and trucks.

tion injury whereas in Los Angeles it is common. The major pollutants are ozone, SO_2, nitric oxides and peroxyacetyl nitrate(PAN).

Finally, much is said about vandalism of plants in cities. However, on the streets of New York the more frequent damage done by cars, trucks, bicycles and urban construction has more severe consequences than the breaking of twigs by people. Trees planted too close to curbs suffer regular injury by motorists.

When faced with all these stresses it is in fact incredible that we have as many healthy street trees as we do.

What can you do to take charge of your trees?

1. Water, water, water. Because of restricted rooting space and increased heat load, street trees often experience water stress — not enough water to meet the needs of the tree. For a small tree you can slowly pour in about ten gallons of water every five days during periods of little rain and/or hot temperatures. However, don't dump spent wash water onto trees when a caustic detergent or bleach has been added to the water. This can cause rapid root damage. It may be necessary to use a fork to gently loosen the soil

Ivy, daffodils and other plants in a street tree pit help discourage visits by dogs.

you to water the ground (i.e. the tree), and may help discourage the parking of bicycles and trash cans at the tree's base. It will also help prevent further soil compaction. In some instances, ground covers may also discourage dogs. While occasional dog "visits" should not harm the tree, excessive dog urine can be toxic to tree roots.

4. What can you do about deicing salts and trees? If you are the perpetrator, begin using sand on your sidewalk or even a small amount of granular fertilizer. Both of these are better than salt. In any case, shovel salt-laden snow away from tree roots. In late winter or early spring when the soil has thawed, flush any remaining salts through the soil by watering with at least 10 to 20 gallons of water.

5. Become involved. Take a course or teach yourself the proper way to prune young trees so that you may remove broken, dead or crossing branches, competing leaders and basal suckers around the tree trunk to insure healthy, vigorous growth.

Enjoy your trees. Appreciate how they give character to your neighborhood, how they make it bearably cool in summer and shield you from wind in the winter. While they produce necessary oxygen, they also trap dust particles, provide habitats for birds and buffer street noise. The livability of our cities is directly related to the health and vigor of our street trees.

surface to about a two-inch depth so that water can be more easily absorbed.

2. Keep the soil around the tree free of garbage, trash cans, bicycles or construction materials. This will help protect the trunk from abrasion and protect the soil surface so that oxygen can freely move into the soil and to the roots. Also, do not add soil on top of the root zone. *Do* mulch the soil surface in at least a three-foot radius around the tree with coarse shredded bark or wood chips. This helps to retain moisture needed for tree growth and reduces compaction around the base of the tree.

3. Should you plant ground covers around the tree? Yes and no. No, because these plants will compete with tree roots for much needed water and nutrients. Yes, because the presence of small flowering annuals such as impatiens will remind

Acer campestre
(Hedge maple)

Zone 4. 25-35', rounded. Tolerates varied conditions, including high soil pH. Relatively pest free; easy to transplant. Moderate to good soil-salt tolerance.

Aesculus x *carnea* 'Briotii'
(Red horse chestnut)

Zone 5. 40-50', rounded. Adaptable to high pH. Prefers moist, well drained sites. Less susceptible to leaf scorch than common horse chestnut. Red flowers. Fruit litter may be a problem in some areas.

Amelanchier
(Serviceberry)
'Autumn Brilliance',
'Cumulus', 'Robin Hill
Pink', 'Tradition'

Zone 5. 20-30', upright. Early white flowers. Prefers moist, acid soil but tolerates pH up to 7.5. Good yellow-to-red fall color.

Carpinus betulus
(European hornbeam)

Zone 5. 40-60', upright, oval. Tolerates drought, heavy soil, wide pH range. Intolerant of soil salt. 'Fastigiata' is an upright form.

Carpinus caroliniana
(American hornbeam)

Zone 3. 30', rounded, spreading. Prefers shade and moist, slightly acid soils; will tolerate intermittent drought. Good orange-red fall color.

Celtis occidentalis
(Hackberry)

Zone 3. 40-60'. Pyramidal when young, open and irregular when mature. Tolerates varied soils, drought, high pH, wind, light shade. Salt-sensitive. 'Prairie Pride' reportedly an improved cultivar.

Cercidiphyllum japonicum
(Katsura tree)

Zone 5. 50-80', rounded, spreading. Best in evenly moist soils, protected sites. Does not tolerate compaction, heavy soils. Tolerates light shade. Relatively pest free. Good fall color.

Corylus colurna
(Turkish filbert)

Zone 5. 50-70', pyramidal. Tolerates drought, heat. Adaptable to varied pH. Pest free.

Crataegus viridis
'Winter King'
(Winter King hawthorn)

Zone 4. 20-35', vase-shaped, thorny. Tolerates drought, high pH. Disease resistant. White flowers, good fall color, persistent red fruit.

Eucommia ulmoides (Hardy rubber tree)	Zone 5. 40-60', rounded, wide spreading. Drought tolerant, pH adaptable. Transplants readily. Pest free. Needs full sun. May be marginal in Zone 5.
Fraxinus excelsior 'Hessei' (European ash)	Zone 4. 60', rounded. Adapts to high pH. Borers may be a problem in warm climate.
Ginkgo biloba (male) (Ginkgo)	Zone 3. 60-100', pyramidal when young, irregular when older. Narrow upright cultivars available ('Princeton Sentry', 'Lakeview'). Tolerates high pH, moderate salt. Pest free. Yellow fall color.
Gymnocladus dioica (Kentucky coffee tree)	Zone 4. 70-80', oval, spreading. Tolerates alkaline soils; pest free. Grows slowly at first. Use male trees to eliminate fruit litter.
Koelreuteria paniculata (Goldenrain tree)	Zone 5. 30-40', rounded. Tolerates drought, alkaline soil, salt. Yellow flower clusters in midsummer.
Mestasequoia glyptostroboides (Dawn redwood)	Zone 5. 70-100', pyramidal. Tolerates pH up to 7.0; does not tolerate soil salt. Favors moist sites. Remove lower branches for streetside use.
Nyssa sylvatica (Black gum)	Zone 5. 40-70', pyramidal. Tolerates wet soils; prefers acid soils (pH 5.5-6.5). Pest free; bright red fall color. Difficult to transplant; use small sizes only.
Ostrya virginiana (American hop hornbeam)	Zone 3. 30-50', rounded. Tolerates light shade; pH adaptable; pest free. Prefers moist soils, but established trees tolerate dryness. Very poor salt tolerance.
Prunus 'Accolade' ('Accolade' flowering cherry)	Zone 5. 20', rounded spreading. Best in soil near neutral (pH 6.5-7.5) Rapid grower. Semidouble pink flowers; attractive bark.
Pyrus calleryana (Callery pear) 'Chanticleer', 'Redspire', 'Autumn Blaze', 'Aristocrat', 'Bradford' 'Fauriei', 'White House'	Zone 5. 30-50', rounded, pyramidal. Tolerates drought, salt, high pH ranges. Attractive white spring flowers. Graft incompatibility can be a severe problem. Some varieties no longer recommended because of tendency for limb breakage.

Quercus bicolor (Swamp white oak)	Zone 3. 50-60', broad oval, rounded top. Tolerates temporary flooding, wet soils, somewhat dry soils. Acid soils are best. Poor salt tolerance.
Quercus imbricaria (Shingle oak, bur oak)	Zone 5. 40-60', rounded. Tolerates high pH,drought. Massive trees need adequate space. Use small sizes when transplanting.
Quercus rubra (Red oak)	Zone 3. 60-75', rounded. Tolerates dry, compacted soils. More adaptable to high pH than most oaks. Good salt tolerance. Oak wilt a serious problem in the South.
Quercus shumardii (Northern shumard oak)	Zone 6. 60-80', rounded, oval. Tolerates pH up to 7.0. Easier to transplant than some oaks.
Sophora japonica (Scholar tree) 'Regent' 'Princeton Upright'	Zone 5. 50-70', dense rounded. Tolerates drought, salt, compaction, wide pH range. Fixes nitrogen. Attractive, cream-colored summer flowers.
Syringa reticulata (Japanese tree lilac) 'Ivory Silk', 'Summer Snow'	Zone 3. 20', rounded. Tolerates drought, high pH; intolerant of standing water. Large, creamy flowers. Suitable for large containers.
Taxodium distichum (Bald cypress)	Zone 4. 50-70', columnar when young, wide-spreading and open when mature. Tolerates wet soils and pH up to 7.0. Moderate soil salt tolerance.
Tilia x *euchlora* (Crimean linden)	Zone 4. 50', rounded. Adaptable to high soil pH. Easier to transplant and more drought-resistant than *Tilia cordata.*
Tilia tomentosa (Silver linden)	Zone 4. 60-80', pyramidal. Tolerates high soil pH; tolerates drought and heat better than *T. cordata.* Less susceptible to Japanese beetle than other lindens. Attractive white pubescence on underside of leaves.
Ulmus parvifolia (Chinese elm)	Zone 5. 30-50', rounded. Disease-resistant. Tolerates drought and wide pH range. May be marginal in Zone 5.

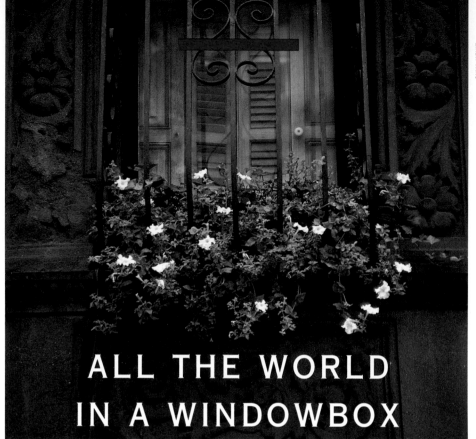

ALL THE WORLD
IN A WINDOWBOX

BY ANNE HALPIN

For city dwellers, gardening often means turning adversities into opportunities. You might, for example, have a small balcony with little sun and lots of wind, or a small, shady courtyard with worn-out soil, or an exposed, gusty rooftop. But you certainly have windows. And if there are windows, you can garden in windowboxes.

This means you can grow flowers and foliage plants for sun or shade, favorite herbs for cooking, small salad greens and other diminutive vegetables, miniature roses, little bulbs and even small evergreens. You can change plants with the seasons for different displays in spring, summer and fall.

A windowbox not only changes the view from inside, it also gives something back to the neighborhood. Boxes full of plants brighten buildings and soften facades of stone or brick with a flash of color and greenery.

If strong winds are a problem on the side where your windowbox will go, concentrate on low plants with sturdy stems and tough leaves. Avoid trailing or climbing vines, thin-stemmed flowers and delicate leaves. And be sure to mount the boxes securely on strong brackets.

Windowboxes have great charm when planted with care and designed with most of the same considerations used in planning an effective garden bed or border. You can create different styles, just as you can in larger gardens.

But whatever the style, choose plants in a gradation of heights to create an illusion of depth and space: the tallest plants in the back, medium-size plants next and low edgers and trailing vines along the front and sides of the box. As a treat for yourself, hide a few smaller plants behind the tallest ones so you

Snapdragons, petunias, lobelia and vinca create a spectacular display.

can see them from inside. That way you won't always have to look at the back of the design.

You might opt for a formal look, with neatly groomed plants in a balanced, symmetrical pattern designed along a straight horizontal axis punctuated by one or more verticals. The plants in a formal windowbox should be balanced in size and shape from side to side and from front to back. If the box contains more than one vertical plant, space them out evenly along its length. The plants in formal windowboxes must also be meticulously groomed, with not a leaf amiss, and this is the place for a small, carefully pruned evergreen, or perhaps a small topiary. To achieve the serenity of a formal design, keep the color scheme simple — perhaps just green foliage contrasted with shimmering white flowers, or a combination of green, white and red or blue.

The formal look is in marked contrast with a romantic, overflowing design. Look for colorful plants that arch gracefully or tumble and cascade. A romantically styled windowbox is full of movement and life. The colors can be soft or bold; the combinations, harmonious and related or a riot of mixed hues. If the windowbox is in bright sun, clear, strong colors look best — pastels tend to fade. On the other hand, pastels and white are ideal for enlivening the shade.

Special effects are also possible in windowboxes. For a tropical look, use a bold-leaved houseplant — *Fatsia japonica,* perhaps, or a young *Dieffenbachia,* a Chinese evergreen (*Aglaonema*), *Dracaena* or Hawaiian ti plant, (*Cordyline terminalis*). Philodendron or pothos can trail over the edges of the box. You might prefer a miniature rose garden, or even a woodsy planting of ferns, primroses and violets.

The size of the rootball determines what will grow in a windowbox. Small plants with modest root systems fare best. These compact plants also work best visually — larger plants may seem out of scale with the size of the box. Think of windowboxes as gardens-in-miniature.

The universe of flowers for windowboxes is surprisingly large, encompassing annuals, perennials and bulbs. Small perennials such as *Iberis sempervirens* (evergreen candytuft) and *Aurinia saxatilis* (basket-of-gold) will perform ably in a windowbox. But for lavish bloom over a longer period, annuals are the way to go. My favorite combinations for a sunny spot are the violet-blue spikes of *Salvia farinacea* 'Victoria' in the rear, silvery dusty miller and verbena in rose, pink and lavender in the center and variegated vinca spilling over the front and sides. (Some of the verbena will tumble, too, as it grows.)

If herbs are your passion, consider anise, dill, fennel or sweet basil for the back of a large box, with thyme or curly parsley for

A SAMPLING OF PLANTS FOR WINDOWBOXES

FULL SUN

Antirrhinum majus — Snapdragon
Arctotis stoechadifolia — African daisy
Calendula officinalis — Pot marigold
Callistephus chinensis — China aster
Celosia plumosa — Woolflower
Centaurea cyanus — Bachelor's button
Cheiranthus spp. — Wallflower
Chrysanthemum spp. — Garden mum, pyrethrum
Cineraria maritima — Dusty miller
Crocus spp.
Dahlia spp.
Dianthus spp. — Garden pinks, sweet william
*Dimorphotheca sinuata — Cape marigold
*Eschscholzia californica — California poppy
*Gazania spp. — Treasure flower
Gomphrena globosa — Globe amaranth
Iberis umbellata — Globe candytuft
Impatiens spp.
*Mesembryanthemum crystallinum — Ice plant
Ocimum basilicum — Sweet basil
Origanum majorana — Sweet marjoram
O. heracleoticum — Greek oregano
Pelargonium spp. — Zonal geranium, ivy-leaved geranium, scented-leaved geraniums
Petunia x *hybrida*
Phlox drummondii
*Portulaca grandiflora — Rose moss
Salvia spp. — Sage
Tagetes spp. — Marigold
Tropaeolum spp. — Nasturtium
Verbena x *hybrida*
Zinnia spp.

*Indicates plants especially tolerant of hot, dry conditions

SUN OR PARTIAL SHADE

Allium spp. — Chives and garlic chives
Browallia speciosa
Buxus spp. — Boxwood
Catharanthus roseus — Madagascar periwinkle
Chamaecyparis spp. — False cypress
Chionodoxa spp. — Glory-of-the-snow
Coleus blumei
Hedera helix — English ivy
Hosta spp. — Small hostas
Hyacinthus orientalis — Hyacinth
Lobelia erinus
Lobularia maritima — Sweet alyssum
Muscari spp. — Grape hyacinth
Narcissus spp. — Daffodil and narcissus
Petroselinum spp. — parsley
Salad greens
Scilla siberica — Siberian squill
Torenia fournieri — Wishbone flower
Vinca minor — Periwinkle
Viola spp. — Pansy, viola, violet

PARTIAL AND LIGHT SHADE

Aucuba japonica — Gold dust tree
Begonia spp. — Wax and tuberous begonias
Caladium spp.
Chlorophytum comosum — Spider plant
Cordyline terminalis — Ti plant
Dracaena marginata — Dragon tree
Fatsia japonica
Galanthus spp. — Snowdrops
Impatiens spp. — Bedding impatiens
Primula spp. — Primrose
Viola cornuta — Horned violet

the front. The middle ground can be filled with small-leaved basils, chives, oregano, sweet marjoram, flat-leaf parsley, sage or coriander.

Salad greens also grow happily in a windowbox. Try baby head lettuces (such as 'Little Gem', 'Tom Thumb', or 'Red Montpelier'), leaf lettuces, arugula, corn salad or

LINDA YANG

Lobelia, geraniums, alyssum and browallia provide colorful blooms and contrasting leaf textures.

mache, sorrel or cress. Or cultivate radishes, round-rooted carrots, little beets, baby eggplant and small determinate tomatoes in your tiny windowbox farm.

To tie your windowbox gardens to the cycling of the seasons, plant in removable plastic liners or individual pots and rotate the plants. For spring, try such hardy bulbs as miniature narcissus, crocuses, scilla and glory-of-the-snow, or such cool-weather flowers as pansies or primroses. Summer can bring some interesting selections other than the ever-popular geraniums, petunias, impatiens and marigolds. There are blue- and purple-flowered *Ageratum, Browallia, Brachycome, Felicia, Nierembergia, Phlox drummondii, Fuchsia, Salvia* and *Iberis umbellata*. Sunny yellows and oranges can be found in nasturtiums, *Anthemis, Coreopsis, Celosia, Arctotis* and *Dimorphotheca*. Some red and pink possibilities are dwarf snapdragons, *Pyrethrum, Verbena*, China aster, *Phlox drummondii*, fuchsias, *Nicotiana, Catharanthus*, Shirley poppy, *Gomphrena, Portulaca* and *Zinnia*.

In windowboxes, as in gardens, autumn seems to be synonymous with chrysanthemums. They are appealing, certainly, and easy to obtain, although best discarded when they finish their bloom. For some-

thing different try colchicums, autumn crocus, dwarf Michaelmas daisies, Japanese anemone or *Sedum* 'Autumn Joy'.

The best soil mix for windowboxes is the same light, porous, well-drained but water-retentive medium useful for pots and other types of containers. It is important to include some organic matter in the medium to aid moisture retention. A good soil mix for windowboxes is one part potting soil, one part crumbled compost, leaf mold or peat moss, and one part vermiculite or perlite. For a lighter weight mix, increase the perlite.

Watering is critical; small containers dry out quickly, especially in hot, windy weather. In some locations you may need to water your windowboxes once or even twice a day in summer. But check first; overwatering starves roots for oxygen and eventually causes them to rot. Poke a finger into the soil. If it's dry an inch or two below the surface, it's time to water. Don't wait until the plants wilt. Water-stressed plants grow slowly and produce few, and poor-quality, flowers. When you do water, water thoroughly.

Fertilize annuals and vegetables every two to three weeks with an all-purpose liquid fertilizer. Most herbs do best with a light monthly feeding, or less. Give shrubs and trees a dose of a balanced fertilizer two or three times during the growing season. Windowbox bulbs need no fertilizer since they are often discarded after they've bloomed. To prolong flowering and keep the box looking its best, pick off spent flowers and dead leaves regularly. ⁂

A large clay pot provides a home for several *Campanula* species,
the graceful bellflowers.

SMALLER MAY BE BETTER

DWARF CONIFERS AND ROCK

GARDEN PLANTS

BY LAWRENCE B. THOMAS

The first considerations for the town and city gardener are space and size. Quite simply, will the tree or plant fit — today, tomorrow and ten years from now?

Some of the so-called "dwarf" conifers can top out at over a 100 feet at maturity, so it is imperative that you research the plants carefully and choose only those that have true dwarf characteristics — forms that naturally are slow-growers, that never attain the size of the parent species from which they derived.

The ones we shall consider here are, for the most part, varieties that are 1) slow-growing; 2) of reasonably easy culture; 3) able to put on a good show for some years without taking up much space; and 4) adaptable to containers and, therefore, useful for terraces and small gardens.

Most of them require at least six hours of full sun, though some of the variegated forms need protection from the hottest sun. All, without fail, do best in well-drained, sandy, acid loam. Fertilizer is rarely needed for the dwarfs since it stimu-lates unwanted growth — although most will respond favorably to an occasional winter top-dressing of manure. Drainage, how-ever, is a prime consideration, and heavy clay soil must be modified with copious amounts of sand, very fine gravel or chicken grit. (The latter is particularly good for container-grown plants.)

When planting nursery-bought plants that have been grown in containers, it is crucial to tease the root ball apart before planting to encourage new root growth.

There are literally dozens of varieties to choose from, and the following represent a mere beginner's list, though there are some selections that should please even the most discriminating gardener. It is crucial when looking for these plants to specify them by their Latin name, for there are many varieties with similar names to confuse the unwary gardener. U.S.D.A. hardiness zones follow each Latin name in parentheses. But check your local arboretum, nurseries or Cooperative Extension Agent for your particular zone.

CEDAR

Cedrus atlantica 'Glauca Pendula' (6) — while not truly dwarf, the weeping blue Atlas cedar is notable for its ghostly gray-blue needles and its graceful, drooping limbs that can be espaliered into interesting forms.

FALSE CYPRESS

Chamaecyparis obtusa 'Nana Lutea' (5) — the dwarf yellow Hinoki false cypress will reach a foot in height, needs semishade to preserve its striking golden foliage and will brighten the darkest corner of your garden.

Chamaecyparis obtusa 'Juniperoides' (5) — a dwarf Hinoki false cypress that forms a tight mound of juniperlike foliage.

Chamaecyparis pisifera 'Squarrosa Intermedia' (5) — this sawara false cypress forms a 20-inch mound of silvery-gray, feathery foliage.

HEMLOCK

Tsuga canadensis 'Cole's Prostrate' (4) — a named variety of Canadian hemlock that hugs the ground and cascades gracefully over a rock or down a slope.

Tsuga canadensis 'Jeddeloh' (4) — another Canadian hemlock that forms a compact, drooping, flat-topped mound with a bird's nest-like hollow in its center.

JUNIPER

Juniperus communis 'Compressa' (5) — The pencil-like growth of this dwarf Irish juniper rarely tops 24 inches, making it ideal for troughs and containers. A nice vertical accent.

Juniperus communis 'Echiniformis' (4) — the prickly hedgehog juniper forms tight little 18- to 20-inch domes.

Juniperus squamata 'Blue Star' (4) — juniper 'Blue Star' forms foot-high spreading mats of steely-blue foliage.

PINE

Pinus mugo (3) — a fine, short-needled European mountain pine that makes an attractive accent in any garden. Among the good varieties are 'Gnome', 'Mitsch Mini' and 'Valley Cushion'.

Pinus parviflora 'Adcock's Dwarf' (5) — a short-needled Japanese white pine that lends itself to pot culture and is often used for bonsai.

SPRUCE

Picea abies 'Little Gem' (2) — a choice rock garden miniature, this bird's nest spruce forms tight little eight-inch buns.

Picea glauca 'Gnome' (2) — this dwarf Alberta spruce grows into dense cones no more than 20 inches high, making it highly desirable.

Picea glauca 'Echiniformis' (2) the hedgehog form of the white spruce is a slow-growing, blue-gray miniature.

Picea omorika 'Nana' (4) — a bi-colored charmer whose needles are green on the underside and blue on top, making this dwarf version of the regal Serbian spruce a real find.

Picea pungens glauca (2) — two good dwarf forms of the popular Colorado blue spruce, 'St. Mary' and 'R.H. Montgomery', are equally desirable.

ROCK GARDEN PLANTS

While rock garden plants don't demand rocks, they do demand perfect drainage. Almost all soil has to be altered to provide this for it is imperative that the plants' roots be able to absorb oxygen. If the soil is heavy, soggy clay, rock plants quickly become candidates for the compost heap.

A good basic soil mix for container growing consists of equal parts (by volume) top soil, peat moss, and a fine (#2 or #3) chicken grit. For plants that require a more alkaline growing medium, small amounts of

Iris gracilipes 'Alba' graces a clay pot backed by several hostas.

horticultural or dolomitic limestone (one tablespoon per bushel) will provide the needed calcium. These lime lovers are indicated by an asterisk (*).

Most rock plants will take full sun. A few, however, prefer part shade and are so indicated.

The following were chosen for ease of cultivation. Most of these plants will respond to basic gardening techniques, while some will challenge the expert — but therein lies the fun.

Aethionema 'Warley Rose', a named variety of Persian candytuft, is a long bloomer that covers itself with pink flower clusters in hot dry positions.

Aquilegia, the beloved columbine, offers many species to choose from. Among the choice rock varieties are *Aquilegia canadensis nana*, a native American dwarf form in red and yellow; *A. bertolonii,* a six-inch Italian gem of purest purple; and *A. saximontana,* a Rocky Mountain endemic with nodding blue and white flowers.

Arenaria montana, the mountain sandwort, is a classic European alpine with white cup-shaped flowers.

*Aster alpinus** serves up lavender to purple flowers in spring rather than fall.

Astilbe chinensis 'Pumila', a handsome pygmy of the genus, delights with clusters of silvery pink plumes that rarely top ten inches.

Campanula species, the enchanting bellflowers, deserve a place in every garden. There are hundreds to choose from, so check names carefully or you may end up with a four-foot surprise rather than the four-inch variety you expected. Some choice ones: *Campanula barbata*, with large one-and-one-half-inch pendant blue bells covered with downy hairs; *C. carpatica,* which forms low-growing mounds of blue or white cup-shaped flowers; and *C. garganica*, an ivy-leafed charmer from the Mediterranean, which explodes into a blanket of purple stars each spring. There are many more, with nary a bummer in the lot. Try many of them.

Chrysanthemum weyrichii produces lovely pink daisies that contrast nicely with the lacy black-green leaves of this sprawler.

Cotoneaster apiculata 'Tom Thumb', as the name suggests, is a splendid miniature that will sprawl over a rock. It is much more accommodating than its thorny big brother.

Find a shady spot for *Cyclamen coum,* which will welcome spring with its shocking pink blooms. Its ivy-leafed form, *C. hederifolium,* will do the same each fall.

No garden should be without at least one of the dwarf daphnes. Try pink *D. arbuscula* or a white form, *D. cneorum pygmaea alba,* either of which will lure the unwary gardener with its seductive aroma.

From the ubiquitous pinks family, choose one of the dwarf varieties such as *Dianthus* 'Tiny Rubies' or *D.* 'Little Joe'. Also try some of the choice bun-forming species such as *D. microlepsis* or *D. simulans,* whose foliage is like a miniature hedgehog until it suddenly blankets itself with bloom.

Dwarf members of the mustard family, the drabas, or whitlow grasses, cover themselves with sharp yellow blossoms at the first hint of spring. Try *Draba aizoides, D. hispanica, D. oligosperma* or *D. rigida* — any one of which will chase the winter blues away.

Dryas octopetala, a mountain avens, endears itself to many with snow-white blooms studded with yellow eyes borne over lush, black-green foliage.

Edraianthus pumilio, a member of the bellflower family, will please the most discerning eye with its uplifted lavender-blue bells over green tuffets of grasslike leaves.

Erigeron alpinus, the alpine fleabane, cheers the soul with hordes of pink or white daisies.

The white form of fairy foxglove, *Erinus alpinus alba,* has long-blooming flower clusters over lacy green mats.

The incredible blue of gentians can lift the heart on the dullest day. There are dozens to choose from, many of them difficult to grow. Some worth trying are: *Gentiana scabra, G. septemfida* and *G. verna.*

Geraniums (not the tender windowbox variety, but the true cranesbill) bloom over a long period. *Geranium dalmaticum,* in either its pink or white form, works magic in sun or part shade.

Also try the sensual, velvet-leaved *G. renardii,* with lovely lavender cups striped with the faintest purple. For a larger variety, look for the inimitable *G. wallichianum* 'Buxton's Blue'.

For a shady corner under shrub or tree, make room for our midwestern woodlander, *Iris cristata,* the crested iris, in either its purple or white form. Plant in rich woodland soil and watch it spread happily — a petite charmer of less than six inches. Leave room for a few clusters of *Iris gracilipes alba* to enchant everyone with white butterflylike blossoms nodding over a six-inch fountain of lettuce-green grasslike leaves.

Also consider the wonderful Japanese roof iris, *I. tectorum,* a beautiful variety whose blooms are less coarse than its long-stemmed, over-hybridized cousins.

One of the glories of the American West is *Lewisia cotyledon,* whose spring show of pink, candy-striped flowers is ever enchanting. A more diminutive relative, *L. pygmaea,* forms a three-inch high cluster of fleshy, fingerlike leaves studded with blooms of pink striped with carmen. More subdued in color, and absolutely ravishing when its apricot-flushed blooms open is *L. tweedyi,* the choicest and most difficult to grow of the lewisias.

Another indispensable family of western wildflowers is the penstemon genus. Also called the beard-tongues, they come in hundreds of varieties which offer many colors and sizes. Look for choice dwarf varieties such as *Penstemon davidsonii,* a low-growing creeper with purplish-blue flowers. *P. rupicola* grows a bit higher and covers itself with bubble gum-pink bloom when happy in hot, dry conditions with full sun. *P. hirsutus pygmaeus* is an easier to grow, well behaved low form with bicolored blooms of lavender and creamy white.

The dwarf phloxes are another American treasure. Forget the ubiquitous *P. subulata*

Chrysanthemum weyrichii produces lovely pink daisies and lacy dark leaves.

forms and search out *Phlox bifida* in either lavender or white. Its lacy blossoms look like intricate snowflakes. Also worthy is our native woodlander, *Phlox divaricata*, a bit taller at ten inches, with several choice lavender-blue shades, and a good white as well.

For shady nooks, nothing beats the incomparable primroses. Look for good color forms of *Primula auricula*, the bears' ear primrose. Or cluster a group of the drumstick heads of *P. denticulata* for instant eye-appeal. And don't forget the sharp yellow of *P. veris,* the cowslip, or another spring harbinger, *P. vulgaris*. Peaty, well drained soil promotes flowering in primulas.

The pasque flower, *Pulsatilla vulgaris,* blooms at Easter in a fine range of colors over a long period, and is interesting when its feathery seed pods waft in the breeze.

There are several distinct types of saxifrage, or rock-foil, each indispensable for gardeners. *Saxifraga* 'Peter Pan' is a choice "mossy" saxifrage, which forms mats of lacelike leaves topped by hordes of yellow-centered white flowers, each petal tipped in hot pink. The encrusted saxifrages have spatulalike silvery leaves that are ringed with white, almost as if they'd been frosted. *S. callosa* or *S. paniculata* are two choices that are stunning even when not in bloom, which is fortunate, for when one of the many rosettes does bloom, it dies. The more experienced grower will seek out some of the incomparable porophyllum saxifrages which form tight little buns of hard foliage and colorful riots of flowers each spring, enchanting everyone. Be forewarned, however, they are difficult, and expensive. Most of them prefer lime, partial shade and perfect drainage.

A final favorite is the common houseleek, *Sempervivum,* sometimes called "live forever." There are hundreds of these rapid spreaders to choose from. One sure favorite is *S. arachnoideum,* with each of its rosettes cobwebbed as if by some industrious cosmic spider.

To find some of these plants, you may have to search out nurseries that specialize in rock garden plants. Do make the effort for these alpine gems and dwarf conifers will help you achieve that oh-so-special garden.

TRY ROSE PETALS & HIBISCUS BLOSSOMS FOR DINNER

BY ROBERT BEALE

How about a rose-petal sandwich, or a cup of lavender tea for lunch? Or for a snack, what about nasturtium pastry, followed by basil blossom ice cream? Certainly this is nothing new, since edible blooms have a long history of kitchen use, not only for decoration but for eating candied, pickled, sauteed or dried. They're an essential part of my eleventh floor rooftop scene and I grow them right alongside my herbs and small vegetables. Which means old roses with basil and chives, and calendula tucked among tomatoes, beans and peas.

One of my favorites is squash blossoms. I enjoy them stuffed with rice, cheese or meat or sauteed in butter or sesame oil. And to add a yellow hue to rice use calendula blossoms. It's true they don't have saffron's flavor — but they also don't cost as much. Daylilies, too, are popular fare; buds, blossoms and roots are edible.

I add rose petals to lightly buttered bread for a tea-time treat. Add nasturtium blossoms and leaves to salads. For flavor and fragrance try blossoms of hibiscus, Johnny jump-ups, pansies, calendula and the petals of roses — the antique ones are best. Remember, the more colorful the bloom, the more colorful the dish.

Another favorite is the scarlet runner bean. This is a quick growing vine with lusty foliage and beautiful, tasty blooms. The bean itself is delicious, and adds zip to soups and casseroles.

The blossoms of many culinary herbs are edible, too. I am especially partial to chives, and use both the flowers and leaves in salads. Both basil blooms and leaves will add a tangy garnish to pastas, and mint flowers will float picturesquely in tea.

Fresh flowers, artfully arranged, brighten any dessert. Candied blossoms of violets and roses are standards for cake decoration and they're easy to find or make at home. The leaves of anise hyssop and scented geraniums are also useful fresh or candied. And try whorls of sweet woodruff or the purple flowers of mint as a topping on mousses and cakes.

Gather the flowers to be used in cooking early in the morning. Wash them gently and store them in the refrigerator, flattened between layers of wax paper or paper towels. Only flowers you expect to use dried should be picked in the heat of the day.

Squash flowers can be stuffed or sauteed in butter or sesame oil.

The flowers of garlic chives are also edible.

Eggplants and tomatoes can be grown in pots but require full sun.

Keep in mind that not all blossoms or leaves are tasty — or even safe. The flowers of four o'clocks (*Mirabilis jalapa*) and sweet peas (*Lathyrus odoratus*) are among the many that are poisonous and some parts of edible plants are toxic, too — such as tomato and rhubarb leaves. Stick to the following list and you'll be safe. Do not experiment in the kitchen.

Remember, too, never use chemicals on what you plan to eat. Also avoid florists' flowers for they may have been sprayed.

Here is a sampling of edibles to grow and harvest in even the smallest garden.

EDIBLE FLOWERS

Anise hyssop (*Pimpinella anisum*)

Borage (*Borago officinalis*)

Carnation (*Dianthus caryophyllus*), (*D.* x *allwoodii, D. alpinus, D. plumarius* 'Spring Beauty')

Camellia (*Camellia japonica*)

Chrysanthemum (*Chrysanthemum* spp.), (*C. parthenium, C. frutescens, C. coccineum*)

Chives (*Allium schoenoprasum*)

Citrus (including lemon, lime and orange blossoms) (*Citrus* spp.)

Dandelion (*Taraxacum officinale*)

Daylily (*Hemerocallis* spp.) (*H.* 'Stella d'Oro', *H.* mixed hybrids)

Gardenia (*Gardenia jasminoides*)

Gladiolus (*Gladiolus callianthus*)

Hollyhock (*Alcea* spp.), (*A. rosea* 'Powder Puffs')

Jasmine (*Jasminum* spp.)

Lavender (*Lavandula* spp.), (*L. angustifolia* 'Hidcote', *L. a.* 'Jean Davis')

Marigold (*Tagetes* spp.)

Mint (*Mentha piperita*)

Pansy (*Viola* x *wittrockiana*)

Passion flower (*Passiflora* spp.)

Pot marigold (*Calendula officinalis*)

Rose (*Rosa* spp.) (*R. rugosa, R. gallica, R. mundi, R. damascena*)

Scarlet runner bean (*Phaseolus coccineus*)

Summer squash (*Cucurbita pepo*)

Sweet woodruff (*Galium odoratum*)

Violet (*Viola odorata*)

Arranging vegetables and herbs in a small space means taking some time first to determine the days needed from seed to maturity, as well as the spacing for good development of each plant. Not every town or city gardener has ideal conditions for starting seeds on windowsills indoors — ideal meaning a full day of sun. So if you plan on starting plants from seed make your selections carefully, or concentrate on varieties that can be sown directly outside after the last frost. I find that soaking seed in a tea solution increases germination by 25 to 30 percent. You'll find that, unlike flowers, vegetables and herbs nearly always grow true from seed.

Many small space gardeners find it's better to wait until later in spring, and purchase flats of nursery grown seedlings to transplant. So even if you started with seed and were not successful, you can start again. And try growing from seed again next year.

Both herbs and vegetables need a porous, well draining soil. In general, veg-etables prefer soil that is slightly acid (pH 6.0 to 6.8) and rich in such organic matter as compost and cow manure (bags of both are available at most garden centers). A handful of bone meal should also be added to each container or per square foot of soil. I like to think of it as a soil conditioner.

Regular feeding is needed throughout the growing season, especially for crops grown in containers (and remember that the bigger the container, the less feeding and watering will be necessary). The three numbers on the fertilizer package denote the proportion of nutrients included, in order. These are nitrogen, phosphorus and potassium. As a rule of thumb, use a high nitrogen fertilizer, such as fish emulsion, for leafy crops like lettuce and a high phosphorus fertilizer, such as bone meal, for crops that set flowers like tomatoes or squash. Follow directions on the package until such time as you can better determine just how often to use fertilizers. You don't want to use too much and take a chance of burning your plants.

Herbs, however, typically are best in a less acid and less rich soil with minimal feeding. If you can, spray all plants with a hose at least twice a week; make sure you do it before the sun is up, or after sundown. You can also fertilize with a foliar spray, such as liquid kelp, once every two weeks.

In any case, plan on rotating your crops. Don't plant the same vegetables or herbs in the same containers or same part of your garden each year. Pretend you're a farmer and aim for a three-year rotation system, at least.

Here is a sampling of vegetables and herbs for the small town and city garden.

VEGETABLES FOR FULL SUN

Arugula (*Eruca sativa*)

Beans (*Phaseolus vulgaris*)

Broccoli (*Brassica oleracea*)

A large strawberry jar is a perfect container for a plethora of herbs.

Cabbage (*Brassica oleracea*)
Carrots (*Daucus carota*)
Cauliflower (*Brassica oleracea*)
Celery (*Apium graveolens*)
Cucumbers (*Cucumis sativus*)
Eggplant (*Solanum melongena*)
Endive (*Cichorium endivia*)
Leeks (*Allium ampeloprasum* var. *porrum*)
Onions (*Allium cepa*)
Peas (*Pisum sativum*)
Peppers (*Capsicum annuum*)
Radishes (*Raphanus sativus*)
Spinach (*Spinacia oleracea*)
Summer squash (*Cucurbita pepo*)
Tomatoes (*Lycopersicon lycopersicum*)

VEGETABLES FOR PART SHADE

Lettuce (*Lactuca sativa*)
Spinach (*Spinacia oleracea*)

HERBS FOR FULL SUN

Coriander (*Coriandrum sativum*)
Dill (*Anethum graveolens)*
Marjoram (*Origanum vulgare*) (*O. marjorana*)
Rosemary (*Rosmarinus officinalis*)
Sage (*Salvia officinalis*)
Tarragon (*Artemisia dracunculus*)
Thyme (*Thymus vulgaris*) (*T. serpyllum*)

HERBS FOR PART SUN

Angelica (*Angelica archangelica*)
Basil (*Ocimum basilicum*)
Bay (*Laurus nobilis)*
Chervil (*Anthriscus cerefolium*)
Chives (*Allium schoenoprasum*)
Mint (*Mentha piperita*)
Parsley (*Petroselinum crispum*)

THE TAILORED GARDEN

TOPIARY FOR SMALL SPACES

BY DEBORAH REICH

Topiary, the training and shaping of plants, is a traditional art that is coming alive again in small gardens. Among the most ancient of gardening arts, topiary has always had its humorous aspect. From Pliny the Younger's ancient Roman villa, where he spelled out his name in clipped boxwood, to the Pennsylvania gardener who turned a juniper into a rabbit, people have used topiary to keep plants attractive — and interesting — within a carefully allotted space.

Types of Topiary

There are many types of plant shaping, both ornamental and utilitarian, that are useful for the limited areas of city gardens. One is the *espalier*. These two-dimensional, vertical designs take up almost no space on the ground, and can be grown in a bed or container one foot wide. Espaliers are invaluable for transforming walls or enlivening fencing, even though they were originally developed for fruit trees in medieval walled towns. There are many formal designs that date to French fruit-growing techniques, including the candelabrum-shaped Palmette Verrier or Palmette Oblique.

Espaliers can also be grown on free-standing supports as living fences or diamond lattice screens, known, respectively, as horizontal cordons and Belgian fences. Freestanding espaliers will conceal a utility area or block a neighbor's gaze without closing off the garden from light and air.

Informal espaliers are a modern American version. These are inspired by a more Oriental look in plant training, and simply stylize the habit of a mature plant. Often one finds a plant in the garden or nursery that has been storm damaged or crowded by its neighbors; a bit of thinning and pruning of projecting branches will create a flat, free-form design.

Knot gardens are composed of miniature hedges that intertwine in patterns. These are especially attractive when viewed from above, making them perfect for courtyards, townhouse gardens or just beyond a picture window or glass door. Fragrant herbs are the plants traditionally used in knot designs. Use different species with contrasting foliage texture and color to highlight the pattern; gray santolina or laven-

Upright junipers are good candidates for topiary. They are tolerant of smog, shade and wind.

der, green boxwood and reddish 'Crimson Pygmy' barberry are an especially attractive trio.

Knot patterns were enlarged and adapted as sinuous, curving designs in French gardens and known as *parterres*. If knots or parterre designs are planted with dwarf, slow-growing plants, they won't need frequent shearing. The spaces between the lines can be covered with landscape fabric to prevent weeds and then topped with a decorative fine-textured mulch such as crushed stone, bark or coal.

A *hedge* is the basic building block of architectural topiary, and the backbone of many successful landscape plans. A row of shrubs or trees evenly spaced and trimmed into a solid line, it can have curved or straight sides but should be wider at the base than the top. This keeps the upper portion from shading the bottom and causing gaps that are as unsightedly as missing teeth in a smile.

If you are lucky enough to have a garden with an existing hedge, there are several ways to make it more interesting. Buttresses can be trained to project from the hedge and frame a long border into separate landscape pictures. Windows can be cut to frame views without sacrificing shel-

TOPIARY CODE: e=espalier; k=knot; h=hedge; s=sculptural; st=standard; p=portable

Alberta Spruce — *Picea glauca albertiana* — s,st
The fine gray-green needles and naturally conical habit make this plant easy to train into cones, spirals, pointed standards and tiered geometric shapes.

Apple/Pear — *Malus* cv., *Pyrus* cv. — e
Fruit trees are easily trained into espaliers, starting with an unbranched "whip." Look for disease-resistant varieties to minimize spraying.

Boxwood — *Buxus sempervirens, B. s. suffruticosa, B. microphylla koreana* — k, h
A classic plant with small, rounded shiny leaves, slow growing and compact. Dwarf edging boxwood and Korean boxwood are good for knot gardens.

English Ivy — *Hedera helix* — e,k,p
More than 400 varieties plus a hardy nature and good growth habit make this plant useful for many kinds of topiary.

Eugenia — *Syzygium paniculatum* — h,s,st
Also called Australian brush cherry, an excellent, glossy reddish leaved plant for Florida, California and Hawaii, with attractive white flowers and purple fruits.

Hemlock — *Tsuga canadensis* — h,s
Sheared hemlock has a velvety appearance. Because of its stature, it is suitable for larger hedges, arches and sculptures.

Hornbeam — *Carpinus betulus* — h
Elegant arches and stilt hedges can be formed from these trees; leaves turn brown but remain all winter.

Juniper — *Juniperus* spp. & varieties — s
The many varieties of upright, rather than spreading, juniper, vary in color from gray to deep green and have a columnar habit useful for spirals and other narrow shapes. Tolerates smog, shade and wind.

Privet — *Ligustrum japonicum, L. lucidum, L. ovalifolium, L. vulgare* — h,s
Small oval leaves cover a fast-growing plant which will recover quickly from pruning mishaps. It may need shearing every other week in the summer and loses its leaves in winter.

Pyracantha — *Pyracantha coccinea* — e,h,s
Semi-evergreen with attractive flowers and berries. A fast grower for espalier.

Yaupon — *Ilex vomitoria* — h,s,k
In southern areas where summers are hot and boxwood will not thrive, this densely textured native plant is an excellent substitute. Use the dwarf form for knot gardens.

Yew — *Taxus baccata, T.cuspidata, T.* x *media* — e,h,s
Dark green, fine-needled texture responds well to severe pruning and shearing.

ter. Long shoots along the top can be trained into sculptural or geometric shapes ranging from swans to finials.

Allow the hedge to be thicker and taller at intervals, forming columns or corner piers, or use a shrub of contrasting color as a terminus. Gold yew *(Taxus cuspidata 'Aurescens'),* for example, has the same requirements as the green variety but adds an element of drama.

Another architectural technique is known as *pleaching.* Branches of adjoining trees are woven together to form a solid wall or canopy. This can be done with trees on either side of a path or gate to create a romantic archway. *Stilt hedges* are rows of trees with smooth trunks and heads cut to form an aerial hedge. These make it possible to add a framework of green without giving up ground. Where zoning restrictions limit the height of walls and fences, a stilt hedge along the boundary adds an additional measure of privacy.

But the topiaries that really excite the imagination and sense of humor are surely the *sculptural* pieces. These may be as sober as obelisks marking an entrance-way, or as amusing as hippos dancing across a lawn. Shrubs that are suitable for shearing into hedges will also work for sculptures. You can start with a young plant, either shaping it by eye or aided by a metal frame. Sometimes the form of an established specimen suggests a subject: a split-top upright arborvitae becomes a rabbit, a spreading yew a frog. Like a hedge, a freestanding topiary should taper towards the top, so that light reaches all portions of the figure and snow loads don't break its branches.

Since a living sculpture requires regular attention over the years, it must be a labor of love, more a mode of artistic expression than a chore. This is a long-term project; the first year the basic shape will be

For topiary spirals consider junipers, which vary in color from deep green to gray.

achieved, but the details and refinements emerge in subsequent pruning sessions. Metal frames have been used for centuries and speed the process along. They are invaluable trimming guides for timid pruners and make it easier to tie branches in the appropriate direction or in complex shapes.

Portable Forms

For temporary effect or instant gratification, there are the portable topiaries. The familiar lollipop topiary is correctly known as a *standard.* A simplified tree shape, it is a single stem plant with a crown of growth at the top. Early engravings show that tubbed standards trained from citrus and herbs were used seasonally to decorate small formal gardens.

With judicious pruning, *Pinus densiflora* 'Umbraculifera' becomes a living sculpture. A mature specimen has beautiful orange bark.

Many nonhardy plants can be trained into standards, and used outside during the summer. Lantana, fuchsia, geranium and heliotrope make lovely flowering trees, while such herbs as rosemary, bay, and myrtle are appreciated for their scented foliage. They add height to flat designs, and are traditionally displayed in pairs on either side of an entrance as a sign of welcome. Standards are an excellent complement to the most ornate or elegant pots and planter boxes.

Metal frames make it possible to quickly achieve simple potted shapes. Vining plants such as ivy can be planted in a pot and twined or tied to a metal frame. Spirals, cones and multitiered geometric shapes are good candidates for this technique. But even more versatile is the *stuffed topiary*, where the frame, which is filled with moss, serves as the growing container for plants. Eliminating the pot means greater freedom in display and faster coverage of the shape, since the plants are on the surface of the form. It is important to remember that smaller and upper portions dry out quickly so plant in the fatter or lower sections only. Then train vining plants to cover the sur-face by anchoring their stems with hairpins or fern pins.

Like standards, these may be too delicate to thrive outdoors during cold winters, especially on a windy balcony or roof garden. Either move them indoors, or store the form in a closet or garage and replant it anew each spring with rooted cuttings or young plants. Ivy and miniature euonymus are fast-covering vines, but don't overlook succulents or sedums for hot, dry locations.

Basic Care

Look after your topiary as you would any shrub subject to the stresses of growing in a restricted planter or urban setting. Well prepared soil is essential for lush, beautiful topiaries, whether they are in the ground or in containers. Weeds and lawn should be kept away from the roots, which should be protected with a light layer of mulch. Do not feed outdoor topiary after midsummer. Late feeding stimulates tender growth which might be damaged by frost. Be sure, too, to remove any leaves or branches that fall on your topiary in autumn or after storms.

Two juniper topiary poodles are the spectacular centerpieces of the Pennsylvania Horticultural Society's urban garden.

LINDA YANG

Pruning

Pruning is one of those mysterious subjects that becomes crystal clear once you've mastered the basic principles. Properly carried out, pruning stimulates and directs growth. Look at the area where the branch meets the leaf — you will see a dormant bud nestled between. If the branch tip is cut, these shoots sprout new leaves and form side twigs. Make cuts on a slant in the direction you want the new branch to grow, just above the leaf bud.

There are two types of pruning: structural and shearing. In structural pruning, larger branches are shortened or removed to establish or regain the desired shape. Shearing is the overall removal of surface shoots so the topiary keeps its dense coat of leaves. The best time to shear a hedge or topiary, a garden adage says, is when the gardener finds the time. Extensive structural pruning, however, is best done during the dormant season or just before shoots appear in spring. The exception is fruit espaliers, which should be pruned in summer to channel the plants' energy away from vegetative growth and into fruit production.

While standards may appear to be the most sophisticated horticultural creations, they are also created from basic pruning techniques. Start with a plant with a strong central stem, known as a leader. When the leader reaches the desired height, pinch out the top to encourage side branches to form a head. Once the head has developed, remove the lower branches.

Trained plants usually need to be tied to a frame, stake or support, especially in the initial stage. It is critical to remember that stems increase in diameter as they gain height and age, so all ties should be checked to avoid girdling, or strangling, trunks and branches. This can cause permanent tissue damage and often loss of limb. Use natural materials such as twine and raffia, so that if a tie is forgotten it may rot before it girdles the branch. Wire should never be used, and plastic and wire twist ties should only be temporary measures.

For topiary inspiration, unleash your imagination and study old garden prints — Europeans have stylishly coped with cramped gardens for centuries. Even a single topiary can transform a small garden into a magical spot.

The poetic silhouette of a weeping mulberry against a blue, cloud-studded sky.

BEAUTIFUL WEEPERS

SMALL WEEPING

TREES FOR

SMALL GARDENS

BY LINDA YANG

Weeping trees — plants whose limbs grow down, not up — are spectacular sculptures in winter and graceful accents in summer. Take, for example, the 150-year-old weeping Camperdown elm in Prospect Park, Brooklyn. It's a mere 12 feet high, but its intricate pattern of branches etch a 25-foot circle.

"What a glorious silhouette it is against the winter sky — it's like no other tree or abstract work of art," said Robert Makla, who, with his fellow members of Friends of Prospect Park, has raised over $15,000 to keep this treasure alive. "It is, after all, irreplaceable," he said. And so this tree has been fertilized, cleaned and pruned with regularity, and wired with steel cables to keep its massive limbs from snapping under the weight of ice and snow.

BEAUTIFUL WEEPERS
FOR SMALL SPACES

EVERGREEN

Weeping Alaskan or Nootka false
  cypress *(Chamaecyparis nootkatensis*
  'Pendula')
Weeping American arborvitae *(Thuja*
  occidentalis 'Pendula')
Weeping blue spruce *(Picea pungens*
  'Glauca Pendula')
Weeping blue Atlas cedar *(Cedrus*
  atlantica 'Glauca Pendula')
Weeping white fir *(Abies alba* 'Pendula')
Weeping eastern white pine *(Pinus*
  strobus 'Pendula')
Weeping Sargent hemlock *(Tsuga*
  canadensis 'Pendula')
Weeping Serbian spruce *(Picea omorika*
  'Pendula')
Weeping white fir *(Abies alba* 'Pendula')

DECIDUOUS

Weeping birch *(Betula pendula* 'Gracilis'
  or 'Youngii')
Weeping Camperdown elm *(Ulmus*
  glabra 'Camperdownii')
Weeping flowering crabapple 'Red Jade'
  (Malus 'Red Jade')
Weeping Japanese dogwood *(Cornus*
  kousa 'Pendula')
Weeping golden chain *(Laburnum*
  alpinum 'Pendula')
Weeping Katsura *(Cercidiphyllum mag-*
  nificum 'Pendulum')
Weeping pussy willow *(Salix caprea*
  'Pendula')
Weeping Siberian pea *(Caragana*
  arborescens 'Pendula')
Weeping white cherry 'White Fountain'
  (Prunus 'White Fountain')

While not every weeper lives long enough to become such a venerable and treasured presence, even a young plant adds distinction to a tiny garden space. When pendulous plants are considered, it's the weeping willow that first springs to mind. But this is a rapid grower that quickly grabs more than its fair share of space. So unless you have acres to spare, the weeping willow is a tree to avoid.

The weepers to use instead are the slower growers or those more easily controlled with pruning. Since the vertical growth of such trees is limited — from two to fifteen feet, depending on the species — these are the plants for small town or city gardens. These are also the plants for patio, balcony or terrace containers, especially when ceiling height is restricted.

When I began wondering why a plant becomes pendulous or drooping in the first place, I turned to Peter Del Tredici of Boston's Arnold Arboretum, who had been so smitten by what he called the "mystery of Sargent's weeping hemlock" that he spent several years studying this species. "Actually, we don't know quite why it happens," he said, "but the weeping form is a mutation." What we do know, he added, is that most plants have a single growing point that remains dominant so that the whole trunk grows vertical and straight.

In weeping trees, this control mechanism is somehow disrupted. "Instead of developing an upright trunk from a vertical growing shoot, weeping trees develop by superimposing one layer of horizontal growth on top of the previous one," he

A weeping birch grown in a large container can grace a patio, balcony or terrace.

said. This horizontal growth pattern is called plagiotropism.

There are many outstanding evergreen and deciduous weeping plants from which to choose. Among the most easily grown of the evergreens is the weeping blue Atlas cedar. This exquisite member of the pine family bears its clusters of silvery blue needles along sinewy, flexible limbs. Allow its drooping boughs to trail outward, as they grow naturally, or loop them around in a corkscrew shape or stretch them horizontally so the young branchlets hang to form a thin curtain.

The weeping flowering crabapple, *Malus* 'Red Jade', a handsome, deciduous plant that adds several seasons of color to the scene, was developed from seed in 1933 by Brooklyn Botanic Garden. Its pale pink spring flowers and brilliant red fall fruits are borne along gracefully drooping limbs.

"A weeping tree is a piece of sculpture — they're not plants to crowd," noted Daniel Taylor, Vice President of Rosedale Nurseries Inc, in Hawthorne, New York, which carries an extensive selection of weeping plants. So whatever weeper you choose, give it the space it deserves — a corner to itself — or position it where it's set off against a lawn or contrasting ground cover.

Among the weeping trees Mr. Taylor is partial to is Young's weeping birch with its white-barked trunk and irregular pendulous limbs, and the weeping Katsura, which has silvery bark and heart-shaped leaves that are reddish-purple when young. Also outstanding, he said, is the evergreen weeping Alaskan or Nootka false cypress, a fairly rapid grower that has an upright

Careful pruning can give a crabapple, a good choice for a small city garden, a weeping habit.

stem but distinctly pendulous limbs.

Although the effect may be similar, in fact there are different kinds of weeping plants. Trees like the weeping hemlock or weeping beech, for example, generally grow on a trunk that is naturally pendulous. On the other hand, trees like the weeping Camperdown elm or weeping spruce were artificially created by grafting a naturally drooping variety onto the straight stem of an upright form of the same genus. This form is called a standard.

The graft union for the weeping portion of a standard may be as low as a foot off the ground — which is where it is on the Prospect Park Camperdown elm — or as high as six feet. And so weeping plants of the same species may have markedly different appearances.

Despite their naturally horizontal growth pattern, pruning is needed by weepers for size control, as well as appearance, said Scott S. Jamison, President of Oliver Nurseries in Fairfield Connecticut, where weeping plants are also much in evidence. And since in winter tree form is most clearly seen, that's the time to prune. The 'Red Jade' crabapple, for example, if left unpruned, will reach a height of about 18 feet, and its branches will extend over a 35 foot circle. But regular pruning will keep the tree comfortable in a much smaller space.

"When you prune a weeping plant it's important to accentuate the cascading form and avoid creating a moplike head," Mr. Jamison said. "Do this by removing crossing branches first. Then, thin the plant by trimming several limbs from around the area closest to the trunk." Tall growers or spreading plants are kept in bounds by removing several outside branches as well.

Among the evergreens he recommends for small spaces are the weeping white fir, which has rich evergreen needles and silvery-gray bark, and the weeping blue spruce, which has blue-green needles. The weeping cherry 'White Fountain' is a deciduous plant that's also a slow grower. Although it may eventually reach 15 feet in height, its pendulous limbs tend to remain within a compact diameter of about six feet.

"In the forest, plants survive by growing up toward light," said Mr. Del Tredici. "This means that in the wild, plants with horizontal growth are easily wiped out. Weeping plants are actually maladapted for survival under such conditions." Clearly, such glorious trees belong in a planned garden where they can be seen and properly savored.

Adapted from "Trees that Droop Ever so Sculpturally," by Linda Yang, which first appeared in The New York Times, *February 1, 1990.*

XERISCAPE COMES TO TOWN

BY VIRGINIA STRATTON

As early as 1921, Florence Yoch designed a garden with drought-resistant plants and species native to her Texas home. At the time this was a rather radical idea. Sixty years later, however, the entire country recognizes that we must manage water wisely. Gardening which uses water spar-ingly is often known as xeriscaping. Xeriscaping is not so much a new kind of gardening as it is good gardening with a new emphasis. Its primary concern is the conservation of water.

Xeriscaping has seven, easy-to-understand concepts.

Planning & Design Your garden should

This lush, spectacular rock garden was created using plants
that need remarkably little water.

*left margin: VIRGINIA STRATTON*

PLANTS FOR WATER-THRIFTY GARDENS

Name		Zone
Acer ginnala (Amur maple), *A. platanoides* (Norway maple)	Tree	4-9
Achillea ptarmica 'The Pearl' (Yarrow) *A. millefolium*, hybds & cvs.	Perennial	4-10
Arctostaphylos uva-ursi (Kinnikinnick)	Groundcover	3-7
Arrhenatherum elatius bulbosum (Bulbous oat grass)	Grass	5-8
Artemisia	Perennial	4-9
Atriplex canescens (Saltbush)	Shrub	4-10
Belamcanda (Blackberry lily)	Perennial	5-10
Bouteloua gracilis (Blue grama grass)	Grass	6-8
Briza media (Quaking grass)	Grass	6-8

Several water-thrifty *Sempervivum* species spill out of a strawberry jar.

LAWRENCE THOMAS

begin with a site study. Whether it's a tiny balcony or spacious rooftop, a sunny front space or shaded back, the goal is to group together plants of like water needs. Make a note of places where run-off occurs — perhaps near a downspout — and turn it to good use by putting thirstier plants here. This is the time to consider how much (if any) lawn you need, and how it will be used. A wooden deck, stone patio or a path leading to a quiet corner can replace unused lawn nicely, and is oh, so much easier to care for. Consider using these turf alternatives in areas where nothing will grow, and include garden sculpture and container plants. Raised beds or terraces create visual interest and can also be designed to channel water to control run-off. If drying winds are a problem, plant a windbreak, which also lessens soil erosion.

Water-conserving irrigation. Next, incorporate a water-thrifty irrigation system in your garden plan — an underground drip, bubble or sprinkler design, for example. Since you've grouped your

Buddleia alternifolia (Fountain buddleia)	Shrub	6-8
B. davidii (Butterfly bush)	Shrub	5-9
Callirhoe (Poppy mallow)	Perennial	4-8
Caragana arborescens (Siberian pea tree)	Shrub	2-7
Celtis (Hackberry)	Tree	3-9
Centaurea (Mountain bluet, Bachelor's button)	Annual/Perennial	4-8
Cosmos	Annual	3-9
Cotoneaster horizontalis	Groundcover	5-9
Crataegus crus-galli (Hawthorn)	Tree	5-9
Dianthus (Garden pink)	Groundcover	4-10
Eryngium maritimum (Sea holly)	Perennial	5-10
Gazania	Annual	5-9

continued on page 80

plants according to water needs, the system can be used to direct moisture only to areas that need it, and in the right amounts. Such watering encourages deeper, stronger root growth and, as a result, greater drought tolerance. It also eliminates overwatering, which weakens plants. In addition, correct watering reduces the leaching of nutrients from the soil, and promotes good pore space for oxygen.

Soil improvement. All this planning will be for nothing unless you improve your soil before anything goes into the ground. Improved soil is fundamental to good water penetration and storage. Because chemicals can reduce the activity of beneficial soil organisms, good organic compost is best. This is especially important in the small garden, where chemicals accumulate quickly. Dig down deep as you add the compost; a deep, spreading root system also resists drought stress.

Limited lawn use. If you must have a lawn, keep it close to the house. Make sure you choose the best exposure; eliminate

Cosmos, potentilla and honey locust are water-conserving choices for a rooftop garden.

continued from page 80

Gleditsia triacanthos (Locust)	Tree	5-9
Hemerocallis (Daylily)	Perennial	3-10
Ilex vomitoria (Yaupon)	Groundcover	7-10
Iris, German bearded	Perennial	2-7
Juniperus (Juniper)	Tree, Shrub, Groundcover	3-9
Kniphofia (Torch lily, red hot poker)	Perennial	5-10
Koelreuteria paniculata (Goldenrain tree)	Tree	5-8
Liatris spicata, L. scariosa 'Alba'	Perennial	2-9
Limonium (Statice)	Perennial	4-10
Linum (Flax)	Perennial	5-10
Mahonia	Shrub, Groundcover	5-10

Perovskia atriplicifolia, Russian sage, is a water-thrifty perennial.

lawn elsewhere, especially on slopes and narrow spaces. These are the places for your favorite ground cover or a rock garden. Although the search for the perfect grass cultivar is never ending ("a triumph of hope over experience" as Dr. Johnson said in another context) there are several new hardy and disease-resistant varieties. Your local water authority can recommend the grass or grass blend best suited to your climate. Read one of the many excellent books on lawn care. Your improved soil will encourage the deep root growth that keeps grass going through a drought. And don't overuse fertilizer. We now know that grass uses nitrogen so efficiently that applying lots of high-nitrogen fertilizer has an adverse effect, creating lazy, shallow roots and poor water absorption.

Mulching. Even the best soil is subject to drying, heaving and compaction, which are stressful to plants. Like people, plants can tolerate a few stressful experiences but not a run of them. Mulching reduces these

Morus alba (White mulberry)	Tree	5-9
Papaver orientale (Oriental poppy)	Perennial	4-9
Perovskia atriplicifolia (Russian sage)	Perennial	3-8
Picea glauca (White spruce)	Tree	3-6
P. engelmannii (Engelmann spruce)	Tree	2-5
Pinus mugo (Dwarf mountain pine)	Shrub	2-7
Pinus thunbergii (Black pine)	Tree	4-8
Potentilla	Shrub	4-10
Rosa foetida 'Bicolor' (Austrian copper rose)	Shrub	5-10
R. rugosa (Rugosa rose)	Perennial	3-10
Salvia sclarea (Clary sage)	Perennial	5-10
Trachymene (Blue lace flower)	Perennial	5-9
Yucca glauca (Soapweed)	Perennial	5-10

stresses as it reduces changes in soil temperature and keeps roots from freezing. Whether you choose an organic mulch that breaks down or an inorganic one that doesn't, be sure it allows good water penetration. A good mulch also inhibits weed growth. Apply organic mulches about six inches thick; four inches will do for inorganic ones.

Maintenance. Deep, frequent watering will be necessary until your plants are established. Usually, one year is enough; sometimes two years of attentive watering are needed. Learn what is recommended for the species you have chosen. Since sprinkler systems lose up to 70 percent of their output in evaporation on a dry windy day, water between midnight and sunup. Remember, too, to turn off your system when it rains, and adjust it seasonally.

Low-water-use plants. Drought-resistant plants native to arid and semi-arid climates are best suited to California, the Desert Southwest and other very dry regions. More humid areas will require their own lists of appropriate plants. The accompanying plant list should be seen only as a starting point. The water needs of even these drought-tolerant plants vary widely. For a more precise list of plants specfically for your area, consult The National Wildflower Council, or a state branch, the botany department of a nearby state university, or your local botanic garden. For general information on water-wise gardening, write the National Xeriscape Council.

THE NATIONAL XERISCAPE COUNCIL, INC.
P.O. Box 767936
Roswell, GA 30076-7936

THE NATIONAL WILDFLOWER RESEARCH CENTER
2600 FM973 North
Austin, TX 78725
Include $3 for shipping and handling.

DIVIDE AND CONQUER

WITH ARBORS AND TRELLISES

BY WILLIAM C. MULLIGAN

An arbor becomes a focal point in an informal garden.

Airy, simple structures of wood and other materials lend a degree of enchantment to the town or city garden that far outweighs the effort or expense. Arbor arches, fences, pergolas (criss-crossing beams supported by columns), seating alcoves, even mini gazebos, bring order to what might otherwise seem a meaningless jumble of plants. As decorative focal points in even the tiniest of plots, these fabrications draw the visitor into the garden and extend an invitation to linger and appreciate the gardener's labors.

And this is to say nothing about practicality. By definition, balconies, terraces and rowhouse gardens invariably challenge their owners to get the most from the smallest spaces. Arbors and dividers may be just what the doctor ordered to solve the most vexing problems of spatial confinement. I am a fan of latticework and rely on the medium frequently in my own designs. It's been a staple of gardens from the time of Louis XIV (when it was called treillage), in no small part because of its ability to perform many functions simultaneously. Besides adding decorative charm, a lattice wall or fence shelters the garden from harsh winds, ensures privacy from neighbors and vertically showcases rambling branches and vines.

A crucial advantage of lattice is its ability to create the illusion of greater space. For example, the wooden laths can be aligned so they appear to be radiating from a disappearing perspective. Apply the design to a blank wall at the end or sides of the garden, and the space magically extends itself, even more so if a mirror is added.

A lattice wall adds decorative charm, shelters the garden from harsh winds, ensures privacy and showcases rambling and climbing plants.

WILLIAM MULLIGAN

fence, my friend white-washed it and I constructed a series of four-by-six-foot diamond-pattern lattice panels. These were painted blue-green and hung on nails driven into the fencing. The effect was miraculous — decorative as well as practical. The latticework, which now supports bowers of ivy and morning glory in summer, may be lifted off the nails easily when repainting is required.

In another case, a client who lives in a brownstone asked me to design a tool shed for his backyard. At the far end of the plot was a large, vigorous wisteria that spilled over from a neighboring garden. To appropriate some of this beauty I designed a six- by six-foot shed with pergolas supported by columns extending from its roof on two sides. The shed now serves two functions — cradling the wisteria and housing my client's gardening tools. At this same site, the rear surface of the three-story

This lattice construction, complete with finials and arched door, creates an inviting entrance to the garden.

A number of years ago, a friend rescued some ancient, discarded lattice from the sidewalk outside her townhouse. Piecing it together, she discovered a trompe l'oeil design which she backed with a mirror, and then applied to an overwhelming brick wall at the end of her French-style garden. The wall was softened and the garden visually extended by twice its size.

Soon after, a next-door neighbor installed an unsightly stockade fence between his yard and hers. To minimize the

brownstone facing the garden was a terrible eyesore, with crumbling brick work and peeling paint. To hide these imperfections and add to the garden's appeal, I covered the entire building with square-pattern lattice, with an opening for each of the windows. After first painting the building dark green, I built the lattice in modular panels and painted it a lighter green. Each of the panels was secured in place by screwing it to metal L brackets that are screwed into the brick. The lattice remains separated by inches from the building's surface, and may be readily removed for repainting.

It's hardly necessary to embark on such an elaborate undertaking to enjoy the rewards of latticework. A small panel inserted into a container to support a vine, or a single panel attached to a wall to accommodate a climbing rose can be just as effective. Once the basic materials are understood, simple lattice construction can be tackled with aplomb by even the most inexperienced woodworker. The basic component, flat wooden lattice (or lath) is available at most lumberyards in widths ranging from three-quarter inch to one and five-eighths inches. Your choice of size will depend on whether you're after delicacy or strength in both look and function. For even greater rigidity, such as might be required for stouter vines like wisteria, you might choose wood sized one by two or one-half by two to overlap lattice fashion.

WILLIAM MULLIGAN

A latticework wall is a distinguished backdrop for a formal urban garden.

Deciding which criss-cross pattern to use — diagonal diamonds or straight up-and down squares — is purely a matter of personal preference. How widely you space the laths will be determined largely by function. Laths spaced far apart, for example, lend a light, airy look, but won't provide much privacy or protection from the wind. Obviously, the latter two considerations demand tightly positioned laths.

To make a simple square or rectangular trellis panel, construct a four-sided frame using one by two (actually three-quarters by one and a half) or one by three (three-quarters by two and a half) lumber. Lay the cut laths across the frame in your preferred pattern and secure them to the frame and each other at the cross points with a heavy-duty staple gun. To cover the lath ends, back the frame, along its perimeter, with more one by twos or one by threes. A series of these completed panels can be nailed to sturdy posts to form a fence or put together as modules to form any number of imaginative configurations.

For the fainthearted, preassembled diamond-pattern lattice panels are sold at lumberyards in four-by eight- and two-by-eight-foot sizes. The lath width on these is one and five-eighths inches, and the panels are sold untrimmed; that is, they must be framed with one by twos, one by threes or specially grooved lumber made for this purpose. Once trimmed out in this fashion and painted, these panels become versatile modular units that can be nailed together in various arrangements to form fences, screens and struc-

A square-pattern lattice painted dark green hides the imperfections of a building.

tures. Be forewarned that these products are pressure treated for weather resistance, meaning that the wood used has been injected with arsenic. Be sure to wear gloves and a breathing mask when sanding or sawing.

At one time, I recommended using only treated lumber, but potential harm to the worker and the environment has prompted me to reverse myself. Instead, purchase top-grade, *untreated* pine and before painting, apply a coat of one of the new low-toxicity, water-repellent preservatives available at hardware stores. This precaution, along with painting all lumber with two coats of outdoor house paint before assembly and repainting at the first sign of deterioration, will guarantee that the work will endure for generations.

My own color preferences for tradition-al lattice construction are white, dark green, light blue-green and gray. Be sure to use only galvanized or concrete-coated nails, staples and metal brackets to avoid marring the finish with eventual rust

streaking. And always provide a footing of brick, concrete or stone for any free-standing structure. Resting on bare earth or lawn exposes the wood to too much moisture, leading to rapid deterioration.

To avoid painting entirely choose one of the hardwoods that naturally develop a handsome silvery patina with time, particularly plantation-grown teak (the harvest of which does not damage rainforests), cedar, black locust, catalpa or white oak. Also popular is the rustic look of structures fashioned entirely of raw twigs and boughs. These can be used to great effect if your city parcel favors this style, one in which your efforts will be centered on choosing and gathering rather than constructing and maintaining. A variety of materials, from bamboo to metal tubing to stonework, are available for enhancing small spaces — all you need is a little imagination.

No matter how simple or ornate your venture into garden architecture, you'll be

This lattice was created in panels so that it can be removed
for painting or repairs.

happier with the result if you map it out beforehand. Use graph paper and draw the plan of your site to scale. Then indicate whatever arbor, bench or fencing seems appropriate for the space. Experiment with spatial relationships until you come up with something that suits your needs. Then draw plans of the structures you've decided upon, making them as detailed as possible, assessing the size and amount of material you'll need.

The details and finishing touches will determine whether your garden structure is a knockout or simply passable. Post finials and other ornamental trimmings are available from such mail-order concerns as: American Wood Column, Brooklyn, NY, (718) 782-3163; Irreplaceable Artifacts, New York, NY, (212) 777-2900; and Classic Architectural Specialties, Dallas, TX, (214) 748-1668. Books offering design inspiration include: *The Well-Furnished Garden* by Michael Balston (Simon and Schuster);

House of Boughs, edited by Wilkinson and Henderson (Viking Penguin); *Garden Furniture and Ornament* (Apollo Books, Poughkeepsie, NY); and *The Classic Garden* by Graham Rose (Summit Books).

For those who prefer their garden structures ready-made by others and for whom expense is no object, there are a number of manufacturers and distributors. The English Garden of Redding, CT, and Country Casual Furniture of Germantown, MD, for example, offer quality-grade, prefabricated trellis panels, posts and arbor arches. These are modules designed to be mixed and matched in whatever arrangement suits your fancy. In addition, a variety of small wooden and metal arbors, panels and archways may be mail-ordered from such catalogs as Wayside Gardens, Smith and Hawken and Gardener's Eden.

Among their myriad recommendations, arbors and trellises are a means of lifting

WILLIAM MULLIGAN

An arbor with *Laburnum*, the golden-chain tree, covers a walkway.
Its dappled shade invites a stroll.

A lattice archway on a snow-covered terrace
creates an illusion of space.

fragrant blossoms to the level of visitors' noses, so no survey of garden structures is complete without some mention of the vining plants that are their very raison d'etre. The first that comes to mind is the rose. Roses and trellises are practically synonymous, and there's probably no more beautiful sight in the garden than bowers of ramblers or climbers in full bloom stretching over white lattice. Other show-stopping flowering vines that are ideal for trellis support, and like roses are hardy in the frostier parts of the country, are honeysuckle, wisteria, clematis, climbing hydrangea and *Passiflora* 'Incense'. Tender tropicals that may be brought indoors in winter are jasmine, *Mandevilla, Stephanotis, Hoya* and most passionflowers. For annuals, try morning glory, moon flower and canary creeper (*Tropaeolum peregrinum*). For non-flowering, rambling green growth, nothing surpasses English ivy. If you prefer a dash of color, try the cultivar 'Goldheart', with yellow-variegated leaves. Another foliage vine with striking color (pink- and white-tipped leaves) is the male form of *Actinidia kolomikta*. And don't forget vegetables. Scarlet runner and hyacinth beans, vining cucumber and indeterminate, small-fruited tomatoes will all happily climb onto trellis structures as they work to supply you with nutritious edibles. ⋀⋀⋀⋀⋀⋀⋀⋀⋀⋀⋀

THE ART OF
BIRD GARDENING

BY PATTI HAGAN

Senior American birdman Roger Tory Peterson characterizes as "bird gardeners" people who sow their gardens "not only with flowers but also with cardinals, orioles, jays, bluebirds, purple finches and goldfinches." I bird-garden almost as much as I flower-garden, getting permissive and allowing a lot of questionable plants — pokeweed, smartweed, nightshade, thistles — to continue in my city garden by way of bird fodder. Bird gardeners also have the habit of putting up bird houses for any birds who'd care to share the address. Usually these are miniatures made in the image of the suburban box — detached dwellings, no row birdhouses, no bird duplexes — except, of course, for purple martin condos.

A couple of years ago I found an A-frame birdhouse out on the street with a neighbor's trash. Not wanting to be responsible for more homeless birds in this city, I retrieved it and relocated it in the old crabapple out back. Possibly because it was rather small — an S.R.O.* — no birds ever moved in. However, nearby in the Dorothy Perkins rambler rose thicket that same spring, I caught a pair of cardinals nest-making with 50 percent man-made plastic fast-food detritus off Flatbush Avenue. Right then I vowed to do my best to get the birds of Brooklyn back to basics: whole-

* S.R.O.: Single room occupancy

English sparrow.

Starlings.

Mourning doves.

Black-crowned night heron, a denizen
of ponds and streams.

some, organic, all-natural nesting materials.

To this end I let dandelions have their powderpuff heads and certain rogue grasses thrive along the bluestone path. I did not dispose of old fern fronds and broken twigs if I thought they could be bird-useful. Even so, this spring, while flipping through a gardening catalog, I was delighted to find an all-natural product called Samson Nesting Material. Six dollars would buy "enough . . . to build 12 nests."

The "sterilized" nesting material arrived, late April, in a cardinal-red box: "feathers, moss, hair, string, cotton" packaged by a company called Wildlife Products (P.O. Box 363, Wisconsin Rapids, WI 54494). There was a lot of copy to read on the box, with key phrases ("Blended to Attract Colorful Songbirds of North America" and "Watch the Birds Build a Nest!") repeated on two sides. The stuff was, the box said, "designed to be perfect for blue-

A house finch perches on a branch of
Cedrus atlantica 'Glauca'.

birds, robins, wrens, chickadees, finches, martins, cardinals and hummingbirds." Since the only species observed nesting in these parts during my tenure have been robins, mockingbirds, cardinals and mourning doves, I was eager to believe that "more than 50 species of North American birds will use this nesting material." After studying "Some Ways to Present Nesting Material," I chose the "Directly on Ground" method, described as "the most natural way for birds." Within an hour of informal presentation, several songbirds *not* mentioned in the prospectus of coming bird attractions hit on the nesting goods. Starlings! Choosy starlings. Very quickly they made off with all the white bird feathers. Nothing else. The robins, cardinals, mockingbirds, catbirds were not interested, to say nothing of any of the 45 other songsters I could wish. (My cat, Be-bop, picked out the string to play with.) Two months have passed, the first broods of robins and cardinals have fledged, and the mound of authentic, old-fashioned nesting material remains directly on the ground between a rock and a hard place, getting more unsterile by the day. Contemplating my backyard wildness, I was puzzled as to why so many songbirds would pass up such good mail-order fixings until I went back to the red box for further reading: "In a yard that is kept 'spick and span' the birds will not be able to find the natural materials they need to build their nests." (Clearly I have the wrong gardening style for the product.)

This insight set me to rummaging in the "Bird Homes" chapter of Margaret McKenny's 1939 book *Birds in the Garden*. There I read: "In the scrupulously tidied garden birds often have difficulty in finding materials with which to build their nests . . . In the modern, well-cared-for garden, every decayed branch has been removed, every cavity has been filled and all dead trees are immediately cut down."

Not so in this modern garden, which tends toward laissez-faire. No way can it be cited for spick and span. The two main trunks of the crab have fallen in the past three years and remain on the horizontal, where clematis and wisteria can engulf them. They are well-rotted and favored feeding stations for yellow-shafted flickers and downy woodpeckers. They also grow lovely rippled fungus borders. Birds have dropped wild multiflora rose seed near the house and now the multifloras have climbed the deck, raddling with the Asiatic bittersweet and making an impenetrable nesting thicket plus producing little red rose hips. (And all along I had the habit of sharing the plush white hair of my late Samoyed, Tofu, with the birds during the dog's awesome spring sheddings.)

And then there's the moss. A while ago, inspired by the Moss Temple in Kyoto, I dedicated a small patch of my garden to moss. I sank a roasting pan and laid on rehydrated sphagnum sheet moss for a moss pond, which soon grew to have thickly moussed, brilliant green verges. Robins make bold to strip mine my moss — it has been the stuffing of countless robins' nests these past five years — such that by early June the moss pond is revealed for the dark blue, white-speckled turkey roasting pan that it is. Never mind.

However, I'm assuming that low maintenance, spick-and-span gardeners are in the majority nowadays. And it is for them that Samson Nesting Material was conceived. The spick-and-spanners can keep their tidy garden ways and still put out the messy stuff of bird domesticity. After all, as Margaret McKenny observed: "A garden without birds would be a semi-desert from the esthetic standpoint."

This article first appeared in The Wall Street Journal *June 29, 1988. It is reprinted with permission of the author.*

CHRISTINE M. DOUGLAS

The house finch is a common backyard bird.

INDEX

Brooklyn Botanic Garden

STAFF FOR THIS EDITION:

LINDA YANG, GUEST EDITOR

BARBARA B. PESCH, DIRECTOR OF PUBLICATIONS

JANET MARINELLI, ASSOCIATE EDITOR

AND THE EDITORIAL COMMITTEE OF THE BROOKLYN BOTANIC GARDEN

BEKKA LINDSTROM, ART DIRECTOR

JUDITH D. ZUK, PRESIDENT, BROOKLYN BOTANIC GARDEN

ELIZABETH SCHOLTZ, DIRECTOR EMERITUS, BROOKLYN BOTANIC GARDEN

STEPHEN K-M. TIM, VICE PRESIDENT, SCIENCE & PUBLICATIONS

KAREN BUSSOLINI

White marguerites flourish on a sun-baked urban terrace.